PUT YOUR PURPOSE TO WORK

How to find fulfillment in your 9-5

KENE ILOENYOSI

Author of *Finding Your Sweet Spot* and *DNA of Talent*

PUT YOUR PURPOSE TO WORK

How to find fulfillment in your 9-5

*Thank You!
Kane*

BOOKLOGIX·

Alpharetta, GA

ISBN: 978-1-6653-0258-6 - Paperback
ISBN: 978-1-6653-0259-3 - Hardcover
eISBN: 978-1-6653-0260-9 – eBook

Library of Congress Control Number: 2021920170

Printed in the United States of America   0 7 1 9 2 1

This paper meets the requirements of ANSI/NISO Z39.48-1992 (Permanence of Paper)

Cover and text design by Lucy Iloenyosi, NeatWorks Inc.

To Lucy

Table of Contents

Acknowledgments

I get to teach and tell stories because of the generosity of those who share their stories with me. Thank you, Poonam, Natalie, Alicia, Gerry, Noel and especially Janet Wynn for helping me tell Dick's story. Your stories have challenged and inspired me more than you can imagine.

Thanks, Monica Scheidt, for joining forces with me again. Your review and edits have made this book much more fun to read.

To my publishing support team at BookLogix, all I can say is that you guys ROCK! From my first book to this one, number three, you've always delivered top-notch excellence in customer service and print excellence.

To my better half, Lucy, I thank God I'm in your life. You bring immense beauty and excellence to everything I do. I write the words, but you bring the books to life with your creativity. I love you.

Above all, I give all glory and honor to God, who assigned purpose before creation and who has given me the talents to do what He's called me to do.

Work in Your Sweet Spot

"Working with high school kids can be tough . . . sometimes brutal; the kids can be unruly, will talk back and really test the limits of my patience, but with all that, there's no other place I'd rather be. In the classroom with my kids, I'm like a fish in water; this is where I was born to be, doing what I was born to do, and I'll have it no other way," said Ariel. As a high school special education class teacher, she was definitely overworked and underpaid, and the stress level in the classroom was often high. Well-meaning friends had suggested she quit and go back into the corporate world, where she was making good money. They didn't understand what Ariel had come to discover; when you finally find the type of work you were born to do, comfort, money, security, etc. no longer become your top priority. She had found her purpose and was working in her sweet spot. Nothing was going to take her out of it.

Most people admire, even envy, the likes of Ariel, who seem to have a clarity of purpose and know what they want to do with their lives. Most people lack this clarity and seem to be in an endless search for a better job. And this is the problem: people are looking for a good job, the ideal job, instead of first figuring out their purpose, why they are here on earth. When you understand your purpose, the work you pursue becomes the channel through which you express that purpose.

What This Book Is About

This is a book about purpose and work, written to help the reader get on the path to discovering and working in their purpose.

I have spoken, coached, and written on the importance of working in your sweet spot since 2009. The more I work with people, the more fired up I become with helping others get out of their career rut; and believe me, many people do not like their jobs and the career path they are on. I'm not talking about people in low-income jobs either; most of the people I've worked with have at least a bachelor's, and often a master's degree, and earn between $75,000 and $150,000 a year. Yet, they all were dissatisfied with their jobs/careers. The Gallup organization has studied the global workforce for decades, and I learned about their workforce engagement survey in 2011: 28 percent "engaged," 53 percent "not engaged," and 19 percent "actively disengaged."[1] You would think that the numbers have improved as I write this in 2020, but they are still about the same.

Why? Well, I believe it's because many people have a wrong view of what work is or should be. It is a view of work as labor or activity in which we engage in order to express our abilities, earn an income, and be a productive part of society. All good motives, even for those who have found enjoyable work using their natural abilities, but still lacking in the deepest expression of what work should be. This inaccurate view of work is not always blatant and in-your-face, but often present in our subconscious. The concept of "work-life balance" may have contributed to this view of work, as it seems to categorize work as separate from life, resulting in people accepting whatever level of satisfaction their work offers, be it good, fair, or poor, but then trying to achieve fulfillment in other areas of life—family, friends, community, etc. It is obvious that work is not a separate but an integral part of life, so why should we not equally seek fulfillment at work?

I admit that I have played a part in perpetuating this view, not out of ignorance, but simply by not connecting the dots regarding what work really is. Maybe using the phrase "life balance" instead of "work-life balance" can be a first step in changing this inaccurate view of work.

In 2017, I began pondering on the question "What is work and how should we really view it?" Here's my answer: Work is the expression of our purpose, the reason why we are on this earth at this time. Work is not just about earning an income or adding value or using our gifts. Work is how you and I express, manifest, and fulfill the reason/purpose for which God created us. Till this becomes a foundational truth, we will not fully realize and express our life purpose and will not find the deepest satisfaction work has to offer. And yes, you (and I) were created for a purpose.

> *Work is the expression of our purpose, the reason why we are on this earth at this time.*

Most people have a sense that their lives are for a reason and they don't exist to take up space and just pass time. We are born with certain desires, and one of them is the desire to live a life of meaning. For centuries, psychologists, philosophers, and theologians have written about man's quest for meaning, and most religions in the world share the belief that to each person is assigned a certain destiny. If you've read up to this point, I sense that you share the same belief and are interested in some answers.

My goal in this book is to offer my thoughts on how you can live out your purpose through the work you do. I don't have the answers to everything, but I do have enough to get you started in the right direction.

My Journey
(and Why I Can Write on This Topic)

I started working on my first book, *Finding Your Sweet Spot*, in 2007. The lead-up to this was the desire to speak to and teach others about finding their purpose in life. As far back as I can remember (close to age ten) I have had this sense or feeling that I am alive for a specific reason. I didn't know what it was, but often found myself in conversations about the purpose of life. This became more pronounced when I gave my life to Jesus in 1995 and soon after read Myles Munroe's book *In Pursuit of Purpose*.

Since reading this book, I have owned several small businesses, been a youth pastor, planted churches as a missionary in Zambia, lived in two countries, written two books, and become a career coach and a paid speaker. The one thing that has remained constant is the desire to live out my purpose.

There were many things I pursued and realized were not for me. The journey to living in one's purpose is not a straight path, but one of exploration and taking steps of faith to try new things. As I thought and prayed about living and working in my purpose, and explored my life journey thus far with its highs and lows, I sensed deeply that my purpose is to show others how to discover and live out their purpose through work.

The research that led up to my first book and the abundance of personality and strengths assessments supports the belief that we are all born with certain abilities. We can attribute these to genetics or fate, but the fact still remains that we come out of the womb with certain abilities. As I read up on and interviewed people who loved and found deep satisfaction in their work, the one thing they ALL had in common was the use of their natural abilities in what they did. They did not develop these abilities because of the work; they chose the work because of their abilities.

> **They did not develop these abilities because of the work; they chose the work because of their abilities.**

They chose their line of work because they were naturally wired in a way that made the work a natural fit for them. The abilities come first, not the work. More on this later.

I feel a deep sense of fulfillment during my coaching sessions when my clients see their natural abilities for the strengths they are. As they begin to understand how these abilities influence and determine the type of work and work environment which best suits them, it's as if a veil has been lifted, and they can see a clearer and brighter future. I guess the joy for me at that point is seeing them on the path to fulfilling their purpose.

This book will help you (or at least start you down the path) to discover and live out your purpose through your work. It is a book about purpose and work. So why the Bible references and scriptures? Because I believe that we cannot discuss the truth about purpose and work without talking about The One who created both. That would be incomplete and misleading.

I am a disciple of Jesus. I am not perfect in any way, but I am focused on serving Him by living out my purpose through the work I do. This is why I was created; this is why I am alive and this is what makes me come alive.

Whether you share my belief or not, you will learn a lot from this book about working in your purpose. Enjoy the read.

How to Read This Book

To get the most out of this book, I recommend you keep a journal, a highlighter, and a pen or pencil handy. There are questions and exercises at the end of each chapter, and you may come across a comment or section which will prompt a deeper dive on your part. This is your personal journey, so please explore the paths and bunny trails that arise as you read the book. It will be time well spent.

SECTION ONE

PURPOSE

The Beginning of Purpose

Everything exists for a reason. Everything.

I f you've ever been around a two-year-old for an extended period of time, you may have witnessed their endless capacity to ask the simple question "why." Why do birds fly? Why is the sky blue? Why are you looking at your phone while driving? Why? Why? And more whys.

The innocence of children reveals something very important about human beings: the innate desire for understanding why things are. As we become adults, the focus of our curiosity shifts from why *things* are to why *we* are. Though everyone ponders this, not everyone prioritizes the satiation of this curiosity. The reason we ponder why we are is because there is a reason why we are.

What is PURPOSE?

Dictionary.com defines "purpose" as the reason for which something exists, the why of a thing. So, your purpose is your why—why you exist. To understand your purpose, you must start with the belief that everything has a purpose. Without this foundation, life can be viewed as a vain pursuit of meaningless desires which lead to an empty existence.

For those who believe in the creation story, we agree that there is a reason (purpose) for man's creation and this reason precedes creation. This is important to note: *the reason for man's existence was set out before man was created.* Your purpose was not created for you, but you were created for your purpose. Your reason for existence was set out before you were created.

Life is a bit like a movie. The script is first written with characters developed. Then and only then are actors sought out to play the roles which bring the script to life. This brings to mind the famous quote by Shakespeare: *"All the world's a stage, and all the men and women merely players: they have their exits and their entrances; and one man in his time plays many parts, his acts being seven ages."*[1] The part (or role) you play is your purpose.

Man's original purpose was to manage the earth like God would. This is clearly documented in the minutes of that famous board meeting in Genesis 1:26 (KJV). And God said, "Let us make man in our image, after our likeness: and let them have dominion . . . over all the earth." You and I were created to exercise authority over the earth because we were created in God's image, to look and act like Him—to work, to tend, to dress, and to keep charge over the earth like He does over every other aspect of creation seen and unseen, known and unknown.

If you've never read the creation story, I suggest you do. You'll find it extremely fascinating. I learn so much about life and purpose every time I read it. Let's look at the story of Adam. His purpose was to start the lineage of mankind and manage the earth. To achieve this, he was created with the ability to procreate, the creativity to name the animals, and the ability to work. After he was created, he was assigned to work in a defined spot on the earth. He was given a specific task—tend and keep—to be carried out in a certain place. He was given an assignment that he had been equipped to execute. In this place, there were rules by which he had to live. In this place, he also got to name the animals. He didn't create them, but he named them.

This story highlights five of seven things about purpose.

1. Purpose is specific and generic.

Let's be clear, my thoughts about purpose are influenced by my faith. I believe the world and everything in it was created by God. With this in mind, I believe that there is a specific and a generic purpose for our being. The generic first—all things were created to reflect the glory of God. Humans were created to look and act like God on this earth. I still wonder why creation was necessary in the first place; alas, I have no answers to that. What I do know is that God had a Grand Plan in mind when He started to create.

In 2002, Rick Warren wrote a bestseller titled *The Purpose Driven Life*, and the bottom line in his book is that we were all "created by God for God."[2] If you are The Creator, well, it means that you create; you make things. The generic nature of purpose is that we are created to reflect and bring glory to God.

Within the Grand Plan of creation lies your specific purpose. Again, when you read the creation story, you see that everything created seems to fit into and play a role in a bigger plot. Each of us has a part to play in this Grand Plan, and this is your specific purpose. Your specific purpose is intricately connected to the specific purposes of others and vice versa. No person exists alone; we all need each other. This interconnectedness is the reason why it is critical that we find and live out our purpose.

You are not some random person strolling through life; there is a part in the script of creation that has your name attached to it, and no one else can fill your spot.

2. Your purpose is something you are naturally equipped to accomplish.

I love airplanes and love to fly in them. To watch a 747 or C-130 landing or taking off simply leaves one in awe; there is such grace and elegance to this mass of metal as they glide onto or off the runway. This happens because of thrust generated by the engines and lift created by the angling of the wings (in a nutshell). Every flying craft has some sort of engine and some form of wings; these are required in order to accomplish their task. You would not look at an aircraft and expect it to sail the ocean. (That's reserved for James Bond.)

You are HOW you are for WHY you are.

Just like humans build into their contraptions the capacity and ability to fulfill their tasks, so also humans are born with requisite innate abilities (talents) to fulfill their purpose. We are all born with a unique combination of abilities, and these are not just randomly assigned for the heck of it. Each person is created with a specific purpose and is equipped with the abilities needed for that assignment. Adam was equipped to procreate, the creativity to name the animals, and the ability to till the Garden of Eden. You may say, "Well, that's obvious," and you'd be correct; and in this same way, you also are equipped for your purpose.

I have studied talents and abilities since 2007, and I can say with the utmost confidence that no one is born without naturally occurring talents. According to research done by Johnson O'Connor (founder for the Human Engineering Lab, now called the Johnson O'Connor Research Foundation),[3] most people are born with at least seven talents; many are born with more. Your natural abilities are an indication of what you should do with your life. In my work as a career coach, I have realized that most people use their natural abilities often, but due to ignorance about talents, they don't recognize them as strengths and abilities to be harnessed, developed, and strategically used to achieve a predetermined purpose. You are how you are for why you are. We'll talk about this in Section 3 of the book.

3. Your purpose is part of a larger plan.

God created the world in such a way that everything depends on other things for its existence; this is how life works. Plants create the oxygen needed by humans and animals, and we produce the carbon dioxide they need for photosynthesis. Remember the food chain in elementary science? We are part of this ecosystem and we need each other for basic survival. Adam and Eve needed the plants and animals for food and would have been responsible for taking care of the plants and animals as well.

Your life is part of a larger plan. Life can be viewed as this very complex jigsaw puzzle, and each person is a unique piece. The puzzle is not static but fluid, with each piece fitted in its right place triggering something critical in adjacent pieces.

There aren't two of you, just you. You have never existed, and after you die, you will never exist again on this earth. You are alive, at this time, for a reason. Stop wishing you had lived in another time or were born into a different family or race. You are who you are because you have a critical role to play where you are. My faith teaches me that all things are made with a specific purpose. I believe it.

Teachers teach that pupils may learn. Doctors take care of the sick. Soldiers protect nations. Chefs amaze with culinary delights. Actors and musicians entertain. Scientists discover. Architects and engineers design and build. Writers illuminate and expand our thinking. Name any craft or trade; they serve others. And within each trade lies immense diversity as well.

Your life is not an accident but an intentional act for a specific purpose. We need you to take your place in the big picture.

4. Your purpose precedes you.

God said, "Let us make man . . . and let him have dominion over the earth" before He made man. He set man's purpose before he was made. Think of it like building a house, maybe your dream home. The process can be fun. It starts with a dream about what it will look like—how many rooms it will have, how it'll be furnished, etc. At the dream stage, you may not have even bought the land. Once the land is purchased, then you work with an architect who creates a design based on your dreams. The architect now specifies what types of materials will be used for the different features in the house. All this is done and specified before engineers and builders get to work. Everything needed to build your dream home is specified in the design before a single purchase is made. The design determines what is used and where things are placed.

In similar fashion, and you may not like the way I say this, you and I were created after our roles in the master plan were decided. Remember, we are little pieces in a big plan; the reason for my life was decided long before I came into the picture.

Humans are caught in what I call an illusion of control; we assume we have full control of our lives. This is so far from the truth. Yes, we have been given a measure of control (free will), but sorry, ultimate control belongs to God. Not having full control does not mean we have no responsibility. We do. We cannot escape the consequences of our actions, good or bad.

You were created for a purpose and it is your responsibility to fulfill it. Can God achieve His plan without you? Most definitely. But He has chosen to enjoy your active participation.

5. You have liberty within the scope of your purpose.

I just said we don't have full control over our lives and purpose. That said, within the confines of our life purpose, we have creative liberty. There is a very interesting portion of the creation story that often gets overlooked. Check it out for yourself; it's in Genesis 2 verse 19. When God was done with creating the animals and Adam, He did something I consider quite unusual—he brought the animals to Adam and asked him to name them. What? The Creator brought His creation to another creation (Adam) to assign each a name. And that verse ends with this statement: "and WHAT-EVER Adam called EVERY living creature, that was the name thereof."

What does this mean to me and you? It means that as you pursue and work in your purpose, you have the creative liberty to express your natural abilities. You are a specific piece of a puzzle, and within your fit, you can solve many problems for those pieces that are adjacent to you. In other words, you can do so much for the people you are meant to help with your gifts and abilities. My wife is a good example; she is highly creative, and her mind enjoys solving and simplifying complex problems. These are her strongest talents. She is a graphic designer by profession and works with her clients to simplify and clearly articulate their marketing message before she starts to design their marketing pieces. She also uses these gifts to help nonprofits with the same issue. She uses the gifts to help people redecorate their homes, especially when they have little funds to spend; she helps them rearrange their space, making better use of the furniture and decorations they already have. The same gifts are at work (and purpose being fulfilled), with the freedom to express her gifts in many ways.

The last two points about purpose are not from the creation story, but from my personal study and observations.

6. There are four factors that govern the fulfillment of your purpose.

Through conversations with and reading about people who believe they are living in, or have lived, their purpose, I have found four consistently recurring themes. These factors play a key role in the fulfillment of their purpose.

I. The Direction Factor

The shortest distance between two points is a straight line; and we often wish the path of our life were straight, but it isn't. Like the directions on your GPS from your home to a location in another state, there are twists, turns, hills, and valleys. The key to arriving at your destination is to stay on the right path. This, for many of us, can be a bit frustrating as we battle inner doubts about being on the right path in the first place. Often, when we encounter failure or challenges, we wonder if we made the right decision. I have good news for you—we all go through this whether we know our purpose or not. It's called being human.

In the fulfillment of your purpose, there is the path and the destination. Like the little flower girl at a wedding, her destination is the altar, but along her path, she spreads flower petals. Your purpose likewise is lived out on the path toward a destination. Many people worry needlessly about the destination and end up missing the things they need to do along the path.

What I have learned over time about purpose is that we never get the full picture. You may have the destination but not the path, or you may have the direction but not the destination. Never both. This keeps you dependent on God, The Source of purpose. This is very important, and we'll discuss this in the next chapter.

II. The Time Factor

You were born for a purpose, but for the most part, that specific purpose will not be engaged until a certain time. And the time referenced here is not just a quantity as in days or years, it also includes seasons and quality of time, as in when some other prerequisites have been fulfilled.

The frustrating part to this principle is that you and I don't control the time; we don't know if it's quantity or quality or both. See how little control you have! Our part is to stay on the path of our purpose and to keep learning and developing ourselves, and this leads to the next principle.

III. The Growth Factor

The fulfillment of your purpose requires your active participation, and this cannot happen when you are a baby or child. Active participation requires awareness, which comes from maturity, age, and/or self-awareness. And this comes through growth—an awareness of who and how you are; talents, personality, interests, and the acquisition of complementary skills and disciplines, which will help you fulfill your purpose.

At this point, you may be asking, "Does this mean kids don't have a purpose? Or if someone dies at a young age, was there no purpose to their life?" To these questions and more, I do not have an answer. My goal here is to make you, the adult or mature reader, aware that there is a purpose to your life and to help get you started on the path to finding your purpose. Hopefully, you will pass this knowledge on to your kids and everyone you meet.

IV. The Priority Factor

Your purpose is your life; it's the reason you exist, and thus, it demands your full attention. The path to purpose often starts with a quest for meaning (what's the meaning of life?), and the search often leads one to a certain burden or desire or problem that seems to call your name and demand your attention.

The only way to fulfill your purpose is to prioritize your purpose. There is no way around this. To prioritize your purpose does not mean to live under its tyranny like some artists seem to be with their art or music, but it does mean you make decisions based on how your purpose will be fulfilled. Important decisions like what you do for work, who you marry, where you live, and more; every major decision is made based on how it helps you fulfill your purpose. I know a couple, the Rabes, who left their comfortable life in America to go start a business in a village in Benin, West Africa. They are entrepreneurs at heart who are called to serve others and change communities. They did not want to send money through some aid organization but chose to go live in the community they wanted to serve and start an agro-based business. Their business trains and employs people from this community and supports other local businesses in the area. They have literally transformed the economy of this community. This is their purpose and it's the reason why they live where they are now. Who knows, they may feel a sense to move back home to America or to another country; they are not concerned about that as long as they are living out their purpose.

As long as you similarly understand and apply yourself to these four factors, you will ensure that you overcome the challenges and obstacles (like failure, boredom, doubt, negative opinions of others, conformity, etc.) that you will encounter on the journey of finding and fulfilling your purpose.

7. Your purpose is your sweet spot.

Your sweet spot is where all you are comes together to serve others in a way that brings you fulfillment. It is your gift to the world and where you have the greatest impact. When you start on the path of your purpose, your creativity kicks in. You find that ideas and solutions to specific issues come to you easier. Don't get me wrong, I'm not saying that life in your purpose is a bed of roses; you will have your fair share of challenges. These challenges are often part of the journey and play a key role in your development. I find great joy in working through and solving the challenges that align with my natural abilities.

When you are in your purpose, you birth new ideas and thoughts. Later in the book, we'll talk about the power of working in your purpose. Your impact on life is huge when you are in your purpose.

RECAP: 7 THINGS TO KNOW ABOUT PURPOSE

1. Purpose is specific and generic.
2. Your purpose is something you are equipped to accomplish.
3. Your purpose is part of a larger plan.
4. Your purpose precedes you.
5. You have liberty within the scope of your purpose.
6. There are four factors that govern the fulfillment of your purpose.
7. Your purpose is your sweet spot.

Chapter One Exercise

1. Do you believe there is a specific purpose to your life? If yes, and you know or have an idea what it is, jot it down below or in your journal.

_____

_____

_____

_____

2. If yes, but you don't know what your purpose is, how committed are you to discovering it?

_____

_____

_____

_____

3. If no, why don't you believe there's a specific purpose to your life?

_____

_____

_____

_____

The Source
of Purpose

The purpose of a thing is assigned by the creator of the thing.

For my fortieth birthday in 2012, my wife threw me a surprise party; it was a weekend getaway at a lake house in the North Georgia mountains with some of my closest friends. When we got to the lake house, I noticed a recently shed snakeskin at the bottom of the front doorsteps. This party was about to be over before it started. I was bitten by a snake in 1998, and that was not a fun experience. Since then, I have hated these creatures and often wonder why they were created.

My wife called the owners of the property to report this and request a pest control service right away. Their response shocked all of us: "Yes, there are two black snakes on the property, and they are friendly. Please don't kill them, as they prevent rats from coming onto the property." What? Black? . . . Two? . . . Friendly? . . . Snakes? Are you kidding me? The owners promised they were not poisonous and that we would most likely see them by the pool. I was not thrilled with that answer.

My wife and our guests were satisfied with the explanation and I reluctantly went along. After all, I was bent on having a good time with my friends. At lunchtime, we went downstairs to grill burgers by the pool. And just as the homeowners had mentioned, both snakes were frolicking around under the deck. These things must have been about five feet long each. A friend of mine tried to use the long pool cleaner to shoo them away. One slithered away, and the other seemed like it was having fun with the pool cleaner; it kept rolling around as it was poked. We finally gave up trying to chase it away. It obviously knew its right of occupancy. For the duration of our three-night stay there, we did not see a single rat in or near the house. We had close to twenty people staying there, and we were generating two to three big bags of trash every day, more than enough to cause a rodent invasion. If we had not spoken to the homeowners, those snakes would have been DEAD! And, I guess, the rats would have come back with a vengeance.

I still don't like snakes, but I finally saw a very good reason to have them around . . . if you live in an area with rodents. The owners had a purpose for keeping the snakes on the property.

Where purpose is not known, abuse is inevitable. And to know the purpose of a thing, you have to go the source or creator of the thing (or in our case, the homeowner).

The Ultimate Source of Purpose

God is the ultimate source of purpose, the purpose of everything. Creation did not magically appear on its own; there had to be a start. And I don't mean the Big Bang and evolution. I chuckle when I hear the creationism vs. evolution arguments; it is not either/or but both working together, with evolution working within creation, playing a key role to help species adapt to changing environments.

Creation, however, starts with God, not the Universe, or some inanimate supreme being. Creation starts with a Being whose intellectual capacity and power is beyond what we can ever fathom and understand. Things did not just come to be. Random cells did not just explode together to form this ordered process of nature which is highly predictable as it perpetuates itself. Life-forms reproduce similar life-forms, with anatomies and behavior that have been the same for as long as man can remember. Humans did not evolve from having ears on their buttocks to having them on their heads because they got tired of sitting on their ears and unable to hear in the process.

Creation started with God, The Creator and Supreme Being who is Life and gives life to all creation. Many struggle with this belief because there are many things we do not yet understand. But those things are meant to leave us in awe and wonder and cause us to worship. Many have instead allowed unresolved curiosity to drive them to disbelief, a mindset which says that "because I do not understand, it therefore must not be true." And this same mindset resorts to accepting the theory that there was a Big Bang and cells started to combine to form the higher orders of life over billions of years of evolution. Let's even play out the scenario that it is true: How exactly, then, did those cells come about? How did they randomly organize themselves to form all the highly specialized life-forms that exist? How did these random combinations of cells become predictable in the outcome of the structure and order of their offspring? Cells are a life-form, and I find it hard to believe that something living would emanate from something not living. I accept that these questions can only be answered if you believe creation started with a higher power.

I spend time laying out this foundation because it is critical to you living out the fullness of your reason for being. If you don't believe in a higher power (God) who has a plan in place for everything and everyone, you will either ascribe a purpose to your life which will most likely be wrong, or you will live life responding to whatever comes your way without a sense of meaning. And based on this explanation, we can say there are two types of purpose: self-determined purpose and God-determined purpose.

Self-Determined Purpose

This encompasses visions, dreams, and goals that are determined by the self—either you or someone in your life like parents or a boss. Many people live according to a self-determined purpose, and often achieve great success and sometimes fulfillment from pursuing this. Don't get me wrong. I am not implying that it is wrong to have a vision or set goals for yourself. I believe it is healthy to do so. I am a dreamer and visionary and I enjoy setting and achieving goals. But I do want you to consider the source or motivation behind your dreams, visions, and goals.

As a career coach, I have worked with so many people who had admirable goals, visions, and dreams, and had achieved them, but still they felt empty and unfulfilled on the inside. They were recognized and praised for their achievements, and people wished they could be like them. But on the inside, a number of these high achievers were sad, empty, lacked fulfillment in their success, and yearned deeply for meaning in life. They lived for a purpose (set by self or another), but it most likely was not the purpose for which they were created. It's not what you achieve on the outside that matters, but whether what you achieve is what you were created to achieve. This is the key to fulfillment of purpose.

We did not create ourselves. Why would we then think it appropriate to assign ourselves a purpose? Here are some truths that are greater than you:

- You are part of a bigger plan.
- You have a part to play in that plan.
- You don't know the bigger plan.
- You don't know your part in the plan.

If you don't and can't control these bigger issues, do you see why assigning a purpose to yourself can lead you down a potentially depressing path? You are the created and not The Creator. You are a creator but not The Creator. We will explore your part in the creation process later in the book.

God-Determined Purpose

He who owns it all sets the purpose for it all. Your purpose, your reason for being, cannot be found outside of your Creator. If you want to know the purpose of a thing, you have to ask the creator of the thing.

You were created for a reason, a purpose that fits within a much bigger plan. You are unique, and there is no one else like you. The talents and abilities within you, your family and place of birth, and so many other things are not things you had a say in; you got what you were given. Some may say, "Well, my abilities are part of my genes." And I would agree. And follow up by asking, "How did the gene pool start and how were your abilities selected?" There is a higher power at play here, and He is at play whether we accept it or not.

Science proves the presence of innate abilities, and psychology proves that expertise and work fulfillment happen when we develop our natural abilities and use them in our chosen field of work. I love science and psychology and I believe in both, and I will tell you that both fields support more than they negate the existence of God. Some people may find it difficult to accept the truth that there is a Being who has written out a script for all of lifetime and is creating everything to fulfill that script. If movie and playwriters can do this, it is not a big stretch to believe they mimic the Author and Creator of life.

Your God-determined purpose sets you up for ultimate success in life. Not just external success, but more importantly, deep internal success and fulfillment. If you've ever experienced a state of flow, that is a taste of what it feels like to live in your God-determined purpose.

*A **flow state** (also known as being in the zone, or your sweet spot) is the mental state in which a person performing an activity is fully immersed in a feeling of energized focus, full involvement, and enjoyment in the process of the activity. The concept was named "flow" by Mihaly Csikszentmihalyi in 1975 but has been experienced by mankind since the beginning of time.*[1]

In your God-determined purpose, there is a sense of mission, a deep sense of *This is what I was born to do*, your thoughts and feelings resonating with the reality of living out your reason for being. You feel the sense of finding your place in the big jigsaw puzzle of life. Are there challenges and unpleasant days in your God-determined purpose? Of course. Life is full of challenges—good days and bad days, joys and disappointments. Your God-determined purpose does not inoculate you against these realities of life; it does, however, keep you moving forward with a sense of purpose.

This truth hit me hard again when I read Dr. Viktor Frankl's best-selling book *Man's Search for Meaning*.[2] Frankl, a psychiatrist, was imprisoned in Nazi death camps between 1942 and 1945. His pregnant wife, parents, and brother were all killed, and he endured untold horrors in the camps. Yet, he managed to find meaning within his suffering and move forward with renewed hope. His book has been called one of the most influential books in America. When asked by a young man about his purpose, Frankl responded, "It seemed it was to help others find meaning in life."

Purpose is in the mind of The Creator, and purpose precedes creation. There is a Master Plan and your purpose is in that plan. God determined both. The fastest way to identify your purpose is to seek God. There is great pleasure in identifying and pursuing the purpose for which you were created. You will be happy to know that this is not a tedious process. In fact, there are many things you already know about yourself that may give you a clue to the direction of your purpose. Let's discuss that next.

RECAP:

God is the ultimate source of purpose. However, we can say there are two types of purpose:

1. Self-determined purpose and
2. God-determined purpose.

Chapter Two Exercise

1. If you believe, or you know, there is a purpose to your life, would you say is it self-determined or God-determined? Please explain why you believe so.

_____

_____

_____

_____

_____

2. What do you think of the statement "There is a Master Plan and your purpose is in that plan"?

_____

_____

_____

_____

_____

3. Have you ever played a role on a team, or in someone's life, and had a deep inner feeling that you were in the right place at the right time and offered the right solution? Describe the situation(s), what happened, the part you played, and how you felt about it.

_____

_____

_____

_____

_____

Purpose Determines Abilities

You are how you are for why you are.
Know your how and you can find your why.

read about an experiment in literacy carried out in 2012 by the One Laptop Per Child[1] program. They sent a research team to remote villages in Ethiopia and gave out tablet computers to children without any instructions on how to use them. Would the kids figure out these gadgets on their own? Within four minutes, one of the kids had opened the box and found the on/off switch. He had never seen a device like this before. He showed the others how to power up the gadget. Within five days, the kids were using forty-seven apps per child per day. Within two weeks, they were singing ABC songs in English. The astounding results of this experiment were attributed to two key factors. First, these kids were used to altering objects at their disposal to suit their needs, and they had to make their own toys, unlike kids in developed nations, where a finished toy is often handed to the child.

The second attribute, which is more relevant to this discourse, is how tablets have been designed for use in an intuitive way. They just seem to work with our natural ways of communicating and interacting with the world. This is a common phenomenon with two-year-olds handling an iPhone; they intuitively figure out how it works.

Human beings also intuitively function according to how they are wired. There are several behavioral traits that just manifest in each person, and they often aren't related to the effects of mirror neurons responsible for learning by observation and imitation. These traits are hardwired into our DNA and are revealed as we interact with our immediate environment.

By traits, I'm talking about the innate abilities with which we are born—talents, personality traits, and predisposition to certain interests. We are all born with these innate abilities and they are positively or negatively shaped by the environment in which we grow up.

The purpose for which you were created determines the abilities with which you are born. I mentioned earlier that we each have a unique part to play in this thing called life, and our roles affect and impact others. You have something the world needs, and you need things others in the world have. Thus, life is fully lived when we are engaged in give-and-take relationships with our natural abilities. If you are naturally good with numbers or design or creative thinking, you will find your best fit in a role which requires the abilities you possess.

A number of my career-coaching clients discover that their lack of fulfillment at work is directly tied to being in jobs or roles which require little to no use of their natural abilities. And once they switch to roles in which they use their abilities, they feel so much better about their work and themselves.

I want you to know this: *you were created with a purpose and for a purpose.* Your life is not an accident, you did not happen by chance. There is a specific intention behind your existence, and this intention governs everything about you. Your part is to identify the intention and align your actions with it. And this starts with knowing how you are naturally wired.

Understand Your HOW

Become who you are by learning who you are.
~ Robert Greene

The one key factor which helps people find their purpose (or at least start down its path) is an understanding of how they are wired—talents, personalities, etc. Many people sadly do not have a firm grasp on how they are naturally wired.

For those who get a formal education spanning nursery to under-graduate college, we spend at least sixteen years in school acquiring general and specific knowledge on varying subjects. However, in the subject that matters most, YOU, our educational systems seem incapable of helping us learn about our natural abilities. Much has been written about this deficiency in our education, and yet little has been done to address it.

It baffles me when I speak with people who know so much about technology, space, history, art, and many other subjects but are lost when they are asked about their talents and personalities. They know much about the world outside and very little about the world inside them. Your inner life determines your outer life; who and how you are wired determines how you function with the world.

Whether we know how we are wired or not, we are affected by how we are wired. We can't avoid it. When a situation irks you or a job does not satisfy you or a certain personality type is challenging to you, these are all symptoms of some internal dissonance with how you are wired. But because you don't know the root cause, the situation keeps repeating itself.

You must KNOW THYSELF. Self-knowledge should be a priority for everyone. The more you learn about you, the easier it is for you to live a life that is based on your authentic self.

You must discover what your natural abilities are, identify your personality type, and understand the things that interest you.

You are an amazing creation—one of a kind, unique, complex, and beautiful. I am always awed whenever I read the statement in Genesis 1:27, *"So God created man in His own Image; in the Image of God created He him."* And in the verse before this, He had said, *"Let Us make man in our image, after Our likeness."*

You and I are not God, but we are made in His resemblance. This is my motivation for learning about myself. There should be no greater topic on earth for you to explore than yourself. I hope you will make you a priority.

In my first two books *Finding Your Sweet Spot* and *DNA of Talent*, I wrote extensively on the power of your talents and how to discover them, so I won't go as deep in this book. But I will discuss the key lessons I have learned about talents since writing those books and coaching many people into the right career path.

Things You Need to Know

Your Talents or Natural Abilities

These are ways of thinking or doing things which come naturally to you. Your talent scope can be quite broad, with a mix of abilities occurring at different proficiency levels. Anything you do well naturally is a talent. Talents are not things you learn (skills); they are abilities you are born with.

Seriously, read *DNA of Talent*. I unpack talents in that book.

Your Personality

This is predominantly how you process information and interact with people. We all have natural ways of interacting, and learned ways as well. Our natural manners of interaction are our instinctual responses to external situations. Our learned ways of interaction are patterns we learn by imitating others consciously or unconsciously. We also take on learned patterns when we focus on the negative side of our personality and work to make up for it. Others may also learn certain behavioral patterns when they want to fit in and be accepted within a certain group.

People will often mislabel their personality and that of others because they haven't taken a personality assessment test, or due to ignorance regarding personality traits. For example, many people consider introversion a weakness or something negative. This is wrong. Extroverts are energized by people interaction, while introverts are energized by spending time alone. The reverse also holds true; extroverts are depleted of energy when they are alone for too long, while introverts are depleted of energy by spending too much time interacting with people. Neither is better or less than the other. It is ignorance about personality types that would cause someone to say, "You need to stop being an introvert," or "I need to overcome my introversion." We aren't meant to overcome our personality; we are supposed to harness it.

Unfortunate is the one who works hard to live up to the wrong personality type.

If you don't know who you are, others will assign you an identity, and often it'll be the wrong one. Unfortunate is the one who works hard to live up to the wrong personality type.

Your Interests

These are often overlooked when making career decisions, maybe because interests are considered as things we do for fun. Duh! That's all the more reason why interests are important.

Your talents tell you what you are naturally good at. Your personality tells you how you naturally interact with people. Your interests tell you what is fun for you. If you find something fun—a subject, industry, cause, etc.—and can find a job which require your talents, you will love getting up every day to go to work.

A client of mine was an IT consultant with a strong, creative, problem-solving ability, suitable for consulting. But she always felt there was something missing in her career. The results of her assessment revealed strong musical abilities. Music had always been a key part of her life but was never factored into making a career decision. We decided that she would explore opportunities to use her creative, problem-solving abilities in the music technology space with companies like Spotify, Apple Music, Sirius XM, and other music-streaming services.

Don't discount your interests. They are not just for choosing a hobby.

Your Core Values

These are your non-negotiables. The quote by Alexander Hamilton "If you don't stand for something, you will fall for anything" sums up the importance of having core values. What values do you hold dear? Many people have never really stopped to think through what their core values are. We all have values that are important to us, but have you ever prioritized them in order of most important to least important? Doing this will help you identify your top five, which become your core values.

Core values will help you set some personal boundaries in your life that you will not let anyone, or anything, violate. Core values can also help you in choosing a company to work for. Where talents and skills align, and the candidate and company share similar values, you will find such beautiful synergy in the relationship.

Core values exercises are tough because you have to narrow down to five from a list of as many as thirty to fifty good and desirable values. It is an exercise that forces you to think past what is good to what is a must. You can find a list of core values by doing a search on Google.

Organizations also have core values. I coach part time with an executive communication firm called Speechworks, and fun is a key value of the company. Fun is strategically incorporated into the learning and coaching process with clients and the interaction between coaches. Candidates who are unable to make their coaching sessions fun don't last at Speechworks. Fun makes it easier for coaching clients to work through inhibitions about speaking in public, which is considered the number-one fear in the world, while being recorded on camera. Fun helps them relax and not be hyper self-conscious, which enables them to learn during the session.

The Paths to Self-Discovery

Nothing is truly yours until you understand it—not even yourself.
~ Myles Munroe

This would be an appropriate time to cue music that conjures up adventure in our minds. I believe the process of self-discovery and really looking inward can be one of the most rewarding adventures of life, with immense benefits too. The more you know about yourself, the more equipped you are to move in the direction of your purpose.

The two paths to self-discovery I suggest are assessments and introspection, and it's best to use both if possible.

Assessments

Assessments are tests designed by psychologists to help people identify and understand their innate traits. These tools of self-discovery have been in use for centuries, dating back to Hippocrates in Ancient Greece and the psychologists in the nineteenth and twentieth centuries who came up with theories about personality types. There are tests for personality, talents, interests, judgment, emotional intelligence, and so many more.

Personality assessments are the most common types of assessments used by individuals seeking to learn more about themselves. A few of the more frequently used assessments are DISC Behavior Inventory, Myers-Briggs Type Indicator, the Hogan Personality Inventory, and Highlands Ability Battery.

The Highlands Ability Battery is really an assessment that uncovers natural abilities, and it includes two tests which measure two personality spectra: introvert/extrovert and generalist/specialist. The results are also based on actions you take in response to work samples within a given amount of time, not in response to questions asked. The outcome reveals how you are wired.

There are two abilities assessment tests that I highly recommend: the Highlands Ability Battery and the Johnson O'Connor Assessment. Both rely more on actions taken within a given amount of time than your response on self-report questions. Acting within an allotted time makes it hard for the test taker to skew an answer; you either know how to perform an activity or not. Both tests are based on the research of Johnson O'Connor, the father of modern ability testing. And, in full disclosure, I have taken both assessments and I am a certified Highlands Consultant.

NOTE OF CAUTION:

The results of any assessment are not meant to define you. The results should affirm or confirm something that already exists in you, something you already know, or something you've experienced but not identified as a natural trait. When reviewing the results of an assessment, you should be saying, "Yep, that's me exactly, I knew that," or "Wow, I do that, but I didn't know that was a strength or personality trait." It's amazing how we miss seeing certain things we do as natural traits which are unique to us.

Often when reviewing the results of an assessment with a client, they'll say, "That's a talent? Everyone should be able to see that or do that!" To which I always respond, "Nope! Only people who are wired like you."

The part that really thrills me is when I work with someone who has lived their whole life seeing a strength as a weakness and something to be overcome. I once worked with a lady whose assessment results showed that she was strong at creating processes and developing strategy, and then giving others the space to execute the strategy. Her results also showed that she would not enjoy spending a lot of her time executing the strategies or working on them day to day.

All her working years, her excitement waned once it was time to execute on a strategy she developed. She thought it was a weakness to overcome, as surely, if she developed the strategy, she should be the one to see it to the end, or so she thought. The discovery of her natural abilities gave her the confidence to restructure her team and bring on more people who were stronger at execution and day-to-day oversight. This freed her up to do more strategic-planning work.

When you don't know your strengths and personality type, others will classify you based on how they see you, and not based on how you are. The other danger which I see in career coaching is where people pursue careers based on skill alone and not talents. This is a recipe for burnout and work dissatisfaction.

Assessments are also a quicker way of learning about yourself. Use them, but don't stop there; do a lot of introspection as well.

Introspection

This simply means to look within, into one's own mind, feelings, past, etc. No one knows you better than you, and no single assessment can tell you everything about yourself. Introspection helps you review different phases of your life from childhood to your present, looking for patterns of behavior and action that line up with the results of your assessment. Remember, if something is a trait, there will be evidence of it in your life. Assessments may describe how certain traits manifest; introspection helps you pinpoint if and where they've been evident in your life.

Here's a funny example. Both the Highlands and Johnson O'Connor assessments show that I'm fairly good with numbers. I personally don't like working with numbers and initially dismissed that result as incorrect. Through introspection, however, I realized that I'm often quick with doing arithmetic in my mind, and remembered many times where, for the fun of it, I would add up the numbers on the license plate of cars as they zoomed by. I was adding the numbers before the next car came into view often in less than three seconds. Introspection proved something the assessments were affirming. I thought it was just a clever mental exercise I developed. I still dislike working on the details which go into budgeting and tax preparation.

Our childhoods also have much to reveal about how we are wired, and I guide my clients through an introspection of their life between ages one and ten. (I call this the phase of innocence.) Our natural abilities are neural paths formed in our brain as we developed in the womb. We are therefore born with certain neural pathways (abilities) already formed. As children, we interact with our environment based on how we are prewired; this is often evident in our mannerisms and how we play. Kids, just being kids, manifest their natural prewiring, and this can give the now-adult much to sift through.

Observation is also a method of learning more about yourself and I categorize it under introspection. You observe others: what they do, how they are, and how they relate or respond to you, and most importantly, how you respond to them. Most people don't stop to think about why they respond in a certain way to certain situations or people. We just react or respond, negatively or positively, and then move on. The more introspective we are, the better we get to truly know ourselves—and the easier it is to get to the root cause of any negative reaction or behavior.

RECAP:

To know yourself better, you should know your:

1. Your Talents or Natural Abilities
2. Your Personality
3. Your Interests
4. Your Core Values

Chapter Three Exercise

1. List all the assessments you've ever taken (abilities, skills, interests, etc.)

_____

_____

_____

2. What were the recurring themes in the results of the assessments you've taken? Recurring themes can help guide you toward your purpose.

_____

_____

_____

3. What have you learned about yourself from all the assessments you've taken?

_____

_____

_____

4. Based on what you've learned from all the assessments you've taken, do you have a vague or clear sense of what your purpose is or may be?

_____

_____

_____

_____

_____

Introspection Exercise: Write Your "Life Story"

Look back at your life and document all you can remember: significant moments, high points, low points, fun memories that have meaning to you. Think as far back as you can remember. Use bullet points so it doesn't feel like an overwhelming exercise but go into detail where you want to or feel you should.

As you write, highlight events or situations where you manifested things revealed in your assessments. Note the recurring patterns in your life.

_____

_____

_____

_____

_____

_____

_____

_____

_____

_____

_____

_____

_____

_____

_____

_____

_____

_____

_____

_____

_____

_____

_____

_____

WORK

The Beginning of Work

In the beginning, God created the heavens and the earth.
~ Genesis 1:1

When and how did you learn about the concept of work? Most of us don't think about this question and the impact the answer has on our life.

My dad was a mechanical engineer and worked for the Nigerian Railway Corporation. As a child, I remember him leaving home at seven in the morning to go to work, often coming home for lunch at 11:30 a.m. and then getting off work between 3:30 and 4 p.m. My dad enjoyed being an engineer, and from the way he talked about work, he also enjoyed working for his organization. I don't remember him ever talking as one who had made a wrong career choice. He seemed to enjoy the challenges that came with his job.

Looking back now, I believe this was where I got the sense that work had to be something you enjoyed and not something to endure. My parents, like most adults, could not have known how my concept of work was being unconsciously shaped more by what they did than what they said. I've worked in a number of jobs just to make money, but I never gave up on looking for my ideal work. It's like a script was written into my subconscious which kept me searching for that ideal career until I found it.

What was your idea of work as a child? I ask this because our concept of work is unconsciously shaped when we are children by the adults around us, what they did for a living, and how they talked about work at home. We are shaped by the environment in which we grew up, and sadly, many people for this reason, have a skewed view of what work should be. To understand what work is or what it should be, we have to go back to the very beginning, to the creation story again (truly fascinating, I tell you).

Work is introduced in the opening statement, the very first sentence, of the creation story. In case you missed it, here's how it starts: "In the beginning, God CREATED the heavens and the earth." Get that? God wasn't taking a stroll, or chilling on His throne or meditating on His grand plans. He was CREATING. The word "create," according to Webster's Dictionary, means to cause to come into being, cause to happen, bring forth. In Hebrew, it comes from the word "bara," which means to shape, fashion, form. Last I checked, making, forming, shaping anything takes some effort (work). So, you can say, "In the beginning, God was working." He was working on making the heavens and the earth and everything He wanted. God worked and is still at work.

So, work started with The Creator. If He works, this tells me that work is a good thing, a godly thing, and an important part of life. Not only does this opening statement tell us the origin of work, it also describes what work should be—a process through which we create, shape, form, or bring forth new things.

 ## Definition of Work:
Work is how you use your natural abilities to contribute your part to the world; it is the expression of your purpose.

Why We Work

Man was created to work like God. Sounds crazy, but it's true. At the famous executive meeting where the creation of man was discussed and decided, God said, "Let us make man in our image . . . and let him be fruitful, multiply, replenish, subdue, and have dominion over the earth." We were created to do five things, and none of the things mentioned sound like play to me; they all require effort—work. This was the desire/plan, and the second chapter of Genesis shows us the first steps. The Creator worked and made man in His image to work as well. Look at the story of the first man on earth.

After the Garden of Eden Inc. was established, Adam was made the chief executive officer and responsible for overseeing the operation of this enterprise. God, the Chairman and Founder, said to Adam in Genesis 2:15, "Hey man, your assignment is to dress (tend) and keep (care for) this organization." To get a true sense of what He was saying to Adam, we need to see this from the Hebrew context; dress (tend) and keep (care for) in Hebrew means to "work hard and guard." Rewritten with this understanding, God said to Adam, "Your assignment is to work hard and guard the Garden of Eden."

When you put all this together, it means that for Adam to "be fruitful, multiply, replenish, subdue, and have dominion," he had to "work hard and guard" Garden of Eden Inc. Put in modern-day terms, the work he did would lead to growth, productivity, profitability, engagement, and positive influence.

The Original Plan For Work

With these first revelations, we see that work as originally intended should be creative, bring forth new things, and be something you immensely enjoy (tend and care). Work was, and still is, an integral part of being human. We were created to work, and our work is to be creative—a fun and creative endeavor that will bring forth new things on the earth.

From the original plan, there would be five outcomes from man's efforts: as they worked hard (tended) and guarded (kept) the garden, they would be fruitful, they would multiply, they would replenish, they would subdue, and they would have dominion (growth, productivity, profitability, engagement, and positive influence).

Reflecting deeper on the words "tend and care," I believe there are two aspects to work. Let's look at each one.

To Tend

This being the root word for tender, it also connotes nurturing through attention. Remember, the Hebrew meaning for tend/dress is to work hard.

I remember trying to grow a mango tree when I was six or seven years old. We had mangoes and other kinds of fruit trees growing on our property, but I wanted my special tree. My tending process started with clearing and tilling the soil on a tiny patch of land to soften it and get it ready for the seed. I dug a little hole, dropped in the seed, covered it with dirt, and watered it every day. I don't know if I planted it at the right time and if I was watering it correctly. I had dreams of a big mango tree that would be special because I had taken care of it. I enjoyed watering it and making sure that little patch of ground was free of weeds. In a few weeks, the seed sprouted, and a tiny plant began to grow. I was so elated at what my diligent effort had produced, and paid attention to this young plant for a few months. As a kid, I didn't factor in that mango trees take years to grow and bear fruit, and my childish attention was soon drawn to something else.

Like the wonder and pleasure of a child diligently nurturing a young plant, hard work as originally intended should elicit feelings of joy and tenderness. Just as I paid careful attention to my tree with eager anticipation of delicious fruit, so we also were created to diligently attend to the work assigned each of us. Our hard work brings growth, increase, yields fruit with seeds which can be replanted; and the cycle is repeated until a tiny seed becomes an orchard. This obviously takes time and effort, but thus should be the way in which we tend to our work, nurturing it over time to yield immense results.

As you diligently attend to your work, growth happens on two fronts: you grow personally, and so does your work output. When you start in a new role or position, you are in many ways a novice. Yes, you'll have some knowledge and ability to help you in the role, but you're a novice to some extent in other ways. In your diligent attention, you become more proficient by acquiring new skills, which in turn increases your productivity. As your capacity and productivity increase, so should your creativity. Remember, work was meant to be a creative process; you are bringing forth new things.

This leads me to the importance of developing yourself through sharpening your natural abilities, learning new and relevant work skills, and keeping up to date with emerging trends in your field so you stay current. As Steven Covey says in *The 7 Habits of Highly Effective People*,[1] you keep "sharpening the saw."

Hard work was never intended to be a drudgery; that started when man was dislocated from his assigned spot and started working on land that was not favorable to him. Hard work is meant to be fun and deeply enjoyed. It should be an outlet for you to express your abilities and create new things.

To Keep

The root meaning of this word is to "guard or protect."

I live in Johns Creek, Georgia, a suburb of the metro Atlanta area. When it comes to termite infestation, the state of Georgia ranks highest in the United States. Knowing this fact, you may be surprised to hear that some people choose not to pay for termite monitoring stations around there home. Even more shocking is the fact that some of these home-owners are surprised and often upset when their home is damaged due to a termite attack. They worked to buy a home but did not care enough to protect that home from termites and other things that can cause damage to the home. Like the responsible homeowners who protect/guard their homes from termite attacks, we are to protect our work, our creative output.

We protect ourselves and our work from two things, distractions and destruction.

Distractions cause you to lose focus on what's important. And at work, we know that there are many opportunities for distraction: co-workers who want to gossip, busyness with minor things, trying to do more than you can handle, not having priorities in work, getting into office politics and so much more.

Technology has made distraction more pernicious to the modern worker with social media and so-called collaboration apps pinging and dinging with notifications of latest news and reminders and more. I'm still battling this as I write this book; my cell phone is next to me and I look at it when I feel the urge to. I turn off most of my notifications to minimize distractions but will look at texts when they come in. I love what I do (writing, coaching and speaking,) and really enjoy the buzz I get when fresh ideas pop into my mind as I write. Each new thought feels like turning onto a new path in a forest of wonders; you don't always know what to expect, but you keep exploring. Soon enough, a simple thought expands to a few lines and then a paragraph and soon a chapter. I am more productive and creative when I put my phone away or on silent and ignore other distractions.

> *Chase two rabbits and you'll catch none.*
> *~ Chinese proverb*

The average worker today does not like their job and would rather be doing something else. They are at work because they need the paycheck. Distractions for this type of worker become a welcomed respite from a job they don't like. They love to hit the refresh button on their email and other social media outlets to see what's new. It's like they are saying, "Please show me something new so I don't have to go back to work." Can you imagine how much productivity is lost due to distractions? Guard against distractions.

Destruction may sound extreme when mentioned with work, but hang with me for a minute.

Termite damage to a home does not happen overnight but over a period of time. A single termite colony can eat a pound of wood a day. This is not much. But over months and years, the structural integrity of an infested home becomes compromised. The termites were busy working while the homeowner was negligent and ignorant. When a house is damaged by termites, we should not blame the termites. They are simply doing what they were created to do, which is feed on wood. In the forest, they play their part in maintaining balance in the ecosystem. When a home is built with wood and drywall on land that used to be a forest, the termites don't know the difference; they are just eating wood, which is part of someone's home. The negligent homeowner fails to protect their home with termite bait. And for this reason, insurance companies will not pay for termite damage repair if a homeowner doesn't have a termite protection plan. Think about it, damage from termite infestation can cost close to $9,000 to repair. The annual cost for a termite protection plan is between $350 and $650 depending on the size of the house and where you live. Negligence will cost you at some point.

At work, negligence can mean doing sloppy work, not paying attention to details, sweeping major issues under the rug instead of addressing them immediately, tolerating mediocre work, not addressing poor or bad workplace behavior, and more. When problems are ignored instead of resolved, they fester and get worse over time, and often get out of control. Take sexual harassment in the workplace as an example. Because leaders and boards failed to address it properly years back, many people got away with their offenses, and so many lives and careers were negatively impacted as a result. What you tolerate will grow; what you address will not.

Don't tolerate sloppy work, short cuts, bad behavior on your team, etc.

This is how you guard your work. It is important to you and to others connected to you. Don't be negligent or ignorant about your work; if you are, you will end up destroying your work and life and those of others as well.

RECAP:

1. Work is how you use your natural abilities to contribute your part to the world; it is the expression of your purpose.
2. Work as originally intended, should be creative, bring forth new things, and be something you immensely enjoy.

Chapter Four Exercise

1. Who or what has influenced your concept of work?

_____

_____

_____

_____

_____

2. What unspoken lessons did you learn from your parents or other key people in your life?

_____

_____

_____

_____

_____

3. Why do you work?

_____

_____

_____

_____

_____

4. Do you think your answer above is healthy or skewed? Why?

_____

_____

_____

_____

_____

5. How does your current work life align with the original plan for work?

_____

_____

_____

_____

_____

The State of Work Today

God created work, but we've worked hard to take Him out of it.
Herein lies the dilemma of man.

Work is a good thing, but the state of work today is not good. And by the state of work, I mean how most people feel about their jobs. Proof of this dismal attitude toward work is found in the results of the workforce engagement surveys conducted every year by the Gallup organization, and what people admit when you have a frank conversation with them about work.

Most people in our workforce suffer from **Sunday blues** and **Friday highs.**

Sunday Blues & Friday Highs (SBFH)

You may not call it the same thing, but you know the feeling, and if you don't, you just might be one of the few who love their jobs and are in the right career. Good for you! But for those who don't like their jobs, I'll explain what I mean by "Sunday blues and Friday highs." SBFH is an emotional spectrum with relief (not joy) on one end, melancholy at the other, and anticipation in the middle. Most working adults ride through this spectrum every week, and for many, this emotional ride has become accepted as normal—not ideal, but normal.

Sunday Blues

It's a lovely Sunday afternoon and you are spending it the way you normally do, or maybe you've decided to do something special. You are enjoying the fact that it's still the weekend, but somewhere close to 5:00 p.m., a slight unease settles upon you. Your mind and body unconsciously know you have to go to work tomorrow, and they aren't exactly thrilled about it, almost like mourning the end of the weekend which has become your break from the drudgery you call a job.

These thoughts and feelings are processed so quickly that people often don't recognize the steps; they snap from happy and relaxed to feeling a little blue or anxious. For those who have lived like this for many years, they learn how to maintain a happy exterior and focus on enjoying whatever they may be doing when the Sunday blues hit. Even those around them don't get a hint that they've shifted emotionally.

For some, the Sunday blues means mentally reviewing what your week will be like, the work left over from last week, the negative person or environment you have to endure at work, and you may even sink lower into a negative feeling about yourself for not being able to find a better job, or self-loathing for seemingly accepting the current crappy state of your work life. Some are able to snap out of this by focusing on the good things happening in their lives and whatever benefits this job affords them and their dependents—that "Hey, at least I have a job and can pay my bills" consolation. And yes, it is a consolation because they could be without a job, which bites even more.

Midweek Anticipation

Oh, hump day, how I love thee! I have yet to meet someone who doesn't like Wednesdays, especially Wednesday afternoons. You've pushed through Monday and Tuesday, you've hit the middle of the week, and woohoo, the weekend is in sight! The anticipation of the weekend brings a burst of emotional energy; the knot in your tummy is gone, or at least you no longer feel its effect. Your internal mood lifts; things seem a little brighter and you may have already made plans for the weekend. Whatever the case, the anticipation of a brighter future (the weekend) brightens your day at work. I think people are even happier in Wednesday traffic than they are on Mondays (just my opinion).

It's interesting to note that the little euphoria of the moment dulls our senses to the fact that we'll hit Sunday blues again.

Friday Highs

The relief of making it through another week in a job/career you don't enjoy brings a little high with it. The work week is over, and you don't have to worry about your boss or workplace for two days. This high is not dampened by the impending Sunday blues that will happen again like it has on most Sundays in the past. For now, let's relish the weekend, the time where we sort of get to be our own boss and do what we want to do—whether this is true or not.

This emotional cycle is the norm for most working adults today, and the subtle rise and drop in emotions may be the reason why this state of being has become the accepted lot for many. They work in jobs they don't like and accept work as something to be endured and not enjoyed. Like the frog-in-a-kettle analogy, people who stay in jobs they don't like for longer than they should, will admit it is taking a toll on them mentally and emotionally. But unlike the frog, the environment doesn't kill them, at least not directly.

I will say this over and over again in this book—work is a gift, and we were created to enjoy the work we do.

Why People Are in Jobs They Don't Love

My bills don't care if I love my job.

As a career coach, I have heard all sorts of reasons from people for staying in less-than-ideal jobs. And most of the reasons can be summed up in one word: SURVIVAL. This is at the core of why people stay in jobs they don't like. There are bills to pay, and most people do not want to depend on someone else for their sustenance. I get it. I've been there. But there is a better alternative.

The quest for survival is driven by a scarcity mindset, which echoes to most people that "jobs are scarce, so take what you get and keep what you have." Global unemployment figures seem to support this thinking as well, with no nation being able to claim a 0 percent unemployment rate. Developed nations fare better than developing nations when it comes to employment rates, which leads to an amplification of the scarcity mindset in developing nations. This quest for survival is amplified when resources are, or appear to be, scarce, like in countries at war or where there's severe drought or poverty. This can occur in communities with very high unemployment as result of changing times, e.g. coal-mining communities, or other cities that were dependent on a certain industry that has now become irrelevant or not needed.

The Gallup organization's work engagement survey is really shocking when you realize how many people don't like their jobs and are just in it to earn a paycheck. This is even more shocking when put in the context of more modern times, when people have access to a better quality of life in more parts of the world.

The quest to survive leads to lots of misconceptions about work, like:
- Work is not meant to be fun, it's work.
- Be glad you have a job.

- Working is a sign of responsibility.
- You work till you can retire and then go do something fun.
- Add your thoughts here . . .

When you work based on these misconceptions, you will not find fulfillment and satisfaction at work. Like earlier stated, your work should integrate how you use your natural abilities to serve the world. The work you choose should be based primarily on your natural abilities. When your abilities are not being used, you end up working predominantly from skills you've acquired. This will inevitably lead to burnout and dissatisfaction at work.

Unfortunately, most people are not aware of their natural abilities. This is the root cause of the problem. They may have a sense that certain things come more easily to them, but most likely have not received a confirmation or affirmation about these abilities. When a person does not know their natural abilities, they default to skills and other extrinsic factors for deciding career direction. When we don't know our natural abilities, it becomes easy to believe that there is no defined purpose to our lives. But when you know your abilities, the intuitive next question becomes "How do I use them?" Once a person starts to ask this question, they get on the path to finding their ideal work.

The misconceptions about work are often based on some measure of ignorance, often passed on by the environment in which we grow up— home, school, friends, etc. Yes, we should be responsible, we should be grateful we have a job, and work is often hard, but all that should not stop us from seeking and working in jobs we love. Saturday and Sunday can never fully make up for an unfulfilling Monday to Friday.

LIFETIME WORKING HOURS

Let's assume that we will spend an average of forty-five years working (from age twenty-five to seventy).

45 years = 16,425 days (using 365 days per year)
1 year = 261 weekdays + 104 weekends
45 years = 11,745 weekdays + 4,680 weekends
Days off in 45 years = 1,350 weekdays (assuming an average of 30 days vacation and holidays per year)

Working Years in Days = 16,425 Days

Total Days at Work = 10,395 (63% approx.)
(total weekdays 11,745 - days off 1,350)

Total Days Off = 6,030 (37% approx.)
(weekends 4,680 + days off 1,350)

 Conservatively, each person will spend 63 percent of their active working years at work, and 37 percent of it at home or on vacation.

There is absolutely no way vacation and weekends can make up for the negative effects of working in a job you don't love. And if you drill down deeper into lifetime working hours, you realize that we will spend most of our awake time at work. This further emphasizes the importance of working in a job or career you love. It is much better to come home after a long day at a job you enjoy and reenergize with family and friends than to come home after a long day at a job you don't enjoy and spend time recovering from it and preparing to do it again tomorrow or Monday. When you love your job or career, taking time off refreshes and reenergizes you. When you don't like your job, you take time off to recover.

RECAP:

Work is a good thing, but the state of work today is not good.

1. Most people in our workforce suffer from dreading Mondays and look forward to Fridays.
2. Most people stay in jobs they don't like because of a survival mindset.
3. Vacation and weekends can never make up for the negative effects of working in a job you don't love.

Chapter Five Exercise

1. In your current job/career, are you refreshing and reenergizing at home, or do you use this time to recover from the effects of an unfulfilling job?

_____

_____

_____

_____

_____

_____

2. On Sundays, do you experience the Sunday blues? What time does it kick in and how do you feel?

_____

_____

_____

_____

_____

_____

5 Levels of Work Satisfaction

Alicia's thank-you letter started with, "Thank you for your coaching and helping me return to the field of engineering. I recently started my new job as an environmental engineer with the Land Protection Branch of our state's Environmental Protection Department. I love what I do." She sent me this note after starting her new job.

I started working with Alicia a little over six months before I got this note. A Georgia Tech grad with a civil engineering degree, she got a job in her field right out of college. She loved what she did but soon got tired of the travel required. She and her husband were also talking about having kids and decided that it would be best to find a job that would give her time to be with the kids. Alicia got certified to teach and would spend the next twenty-three years as an elementary and middle school teacher—a job she didn't really enjoy but accepted because of the time it gave her to be a mom.

Well, kids grow up. And hers went off to college. Alicia knew she had to make a change, but being away from civil engineering for so long, she wasn't sure how she'd get back into it. Or if anyone would hire her. Her work was not fun, and she could no longer endure it.

We worked through a process that helped her back into her ideal job, and hence the thank-you letter at the opening of this chapter.

There is an immense sense of relief and revitalization of the person when the work part of their life finally clicks. Alicia's was no different. And as I thought through her experience over the years post-college and that of many with whom I've worked, I realized that there are five levels of work satisfaction, the satisfaction being based on fulfilling the reason for which they started the job.

1. I work because I need a job.
2. I work because I make more.
3. I work because I like my organization.
4. I work because I use my abilities
5. I work because this is my calling.

Level 1: I Work Because I Need a Job

People at this level work out of a desperate need to earn an income. There are bills to pay, maybe mouths to feed, and the job is simply meant to help meet those needs, nothing more. This is the most basic level and reason for which people work, and most people start out at this level. The primary motivation here is survival, meeting current pressing needs. For example, the college or high school grad who no longer lives at home with parents and needs to eat and pay their rent and other bills, or the middle-aged person in a one-income family where every dollar is needed to cover the basic expenses of the home. When kids are involved, the pressure to earn an income is higher, especially where there is little to no money in savings to tide the family over until an ideal job is found.

For those familiar with Maslow's hierarchy of needs,[1] this can be likened to level-one needs, which are physiological needs: food, water, clothing, shelter—pure basic needs. It is often hard to think or work toward other levels if the needs here are not met. Hunger, or the threat of it, is a powerful motivator to get a job, any job, in order to earn an income to buy food. This situation is worse in developing societies with little or no social support services like homeless shelters and food pantries. In developed nations, facilities like food pantries, shelters, food stamps, etc. can help minimize the desperation caused by hunger. Think about this— you can afford to delay paying a bill or two, but you really can't postpone hunger. You can't say, "We won't eat this week, so let's use the money for the gas bill."

When people work at Level 1, it is hard for them to see beyond where they are. They often live paycheck to paycheck, and this causes the vicious cycle of survival to continue. Most people will pass through this level at some point, often more than once. That's okay. The goal should be to move out of this phase quickly, and to not make it their permanent abode.

How to Move Out of Level 1

Working at Level 1 is no fun, and really a rut. To get out of this level, I recommend taking the steps outlined below.

1. Save Money.
Save three to six months' worth of your living expenses, if possible. I say if possible, because there are situations where people aren't earning enough to save that much, at least not in a few years. I have come to learn that no matter how little a person earns, they can always save something. Saving money starts with the right mindset before developing the habit. If you are determined to save money from every paycheck, you will find a way to do so, no matter how little. Once the habit is formed, most people tend to increase the amount they save. This is not a book on finances, and I encourage you to get free resources on budgeting and planning your money. The key to saving money is learning to live on a budget, and planning for every dollar (or whatever your currency) you earn and spend. Whether you earn $500 a month or $500,000 a year, this principle of saving applies: the more you earn, the more money you should save.

For some, the only way they can get to save more money is by earning more. That may mean a second job or starting a business on the side. You may not like the extra work, but it can help you save. Money saved can give you a cushion and buy you some time to find the type of job you really want. It also eliminates the desperation that can happen when someone loses their job and still has bills to pay.

2. Discover your natural abilities.

Don't just focus on saving money; create a plan to move into an ideal job. This step above every other is the key to finding the right job, and I will repeat this recommendation at every level we discuss. You are wired a certain way and will do your best work when you use your natural abilities in your job. Use assessments and introspection as discussed in Chapter 3 to help you identify your natural abilities.

3. Acquire/develop skills and experience.

Your current job requires the use of certain skills for it to be performed well, be it a menial or executive-level job. Some skills are related to knowledge of the job or are task oriented, and others are related to people skills. Make time to list out the skills required for your job and how good you are at these skills. Make the commitment to learn and become good at these skills, especially the people skills. You can use the skills you learn as the foundation to find the next job.

Note of caution here: The goal is not for you to work in your skill area but in your natural abilities. The skills you acquire should support your natural abilities and help you perform better at work.

Level 2: I Work Because I Make More

"More" here includes but isn't limited to money—promotion, perks, benefits, etc. Most people who work at Level 2 are driven by the desire to be secure or safe.

Making more for them means security—financial, social, mental, etc. They get to live a more comfortable life, can save more, do more for their families, etc. It is how they buy peace of mind. Comparing this to level two on Maslow's hierarchy of needs, we can deduce that people working in this level have the sense that more money protects them and is a sort of insurance or buffer from potential dangers in the world.

There are many elements of truth to this; there are so many things you no longer worry about when you have the money to address them. And so, in that sense, it does provide some security, and there is nothing wrong with increasing our income and earning potential. The danger is when the person gets comfortable and stays in or takes a job they don't like simply because they earn more. If they are doing this as a step to moving out of Level 1, this may be okay for a short time to build savings or use this as a stepping-stone to the ideal job. The key thing here is to be mindful not to sacrifice the things that are very important in the quest for more income. I have a friend who moved his family five times to five states in less than twelve years simply because he wanted to earn more money. The constant relocation caused tension at home, as you can imagine. People have divorced over this issue, so please be wise regarding what you'll do in order to increase your income.

Level 2 also includes those for whom the quest for higher positions or more income is tied to their sense of worth; they feel they are worth more as a person when they have more money. This is obviously a very false assumption. Our income or net worth shouldn't determine our self-worth; you are valuable as the unique individual you are. Your value is based simply on the fact that you are you, period. Hard to grasp and believe, especially when we live in a society that ties a lot back to your ability to afford more.

Money can buy stuff, but not the peace of mind needed to enjoy the stuff.

Levels 1 and 2 are similar because they are primarily driven by the desire to meet the basic needs of food, shelter, and security, what we also call survival. Think about this for a minute. Survival is the primary driver and inborn instinct of every creature. From the moment they are born, animals focus on feeding themselves, protecting themselves, and of course, procreating, all in a bid to survive. Man also shares these instincts, but we are expected to live for more than the desire to survive. Many people still live at the survival level and don't know it. With our ability to reason (choice and thought), it is easy to rationalize and come up with excuses/reasons for why we do what we do. There are many high-positioned and financially secure people who still live and work at the survival level. *It is not what you have that moves you out of survival living, but how you think.*

How to Move Out of Level 2

To move out of working at Level 2, do everything I talked about under moving out of Level 1 plus what I add below.

1. Discover your natural abilities.

I told you I'd talk about this a number of times. It's critical. This step above every other is the key to finding the right job. You are wired a certain way and will do your best work when you use your natural abilities in your job. Your natural abilities will determine the ideal work tasks and work environment for you. Use assessments and introspection as discussed in Chapter 3 to help you identify your natural abilities.

2. Invest in a coach.

This is something many people take for granted. If you want to get better at something, you can teach yourself and practice on your own, or you can work with an expert. Working with a coach reduces your learning curve as they guide you to focus on the specific things that can help you get where you want and quicker. I've worked with many business coaches in my life and still do when I need growth in a specific area.

Working with a coach will require an investment of time and money, but also know that there are coaches for every budget range. You just have to look. You can also find coaching resources online or in books.

As a career coach, I've helped many people transition from jobs they don't like to a job they love. They had struggled with this process on their own for many years without good results. Often, by the second or third coaching session, they start to see what and why they haven't been happy in their career.

3. Make a transition plan.

Transitions don't just happen, at least not the ones we really want. You have to plan for and work toward it. For some, the transition may take a few years. When you have a transition plan and you are actively working on it, you can tolerate a not-so-ideal job situation better. Without a plan, it will feel like there is no end in sight to the job dissatisfaction, and this is not a fun place to be. Making a plan starts the process; working the plan will keep you moving toward your goal of being in the ideal career.

Level 3: I Work Because I Like My Organization

Most situations are tolerable when we like the people around us.

"If you don't really like your job, why have you stayed so long at your company?" I asked.

"I like the people I work with," replied Anna. She was an administrative assistant at a regional office of a Fortune 500 company that provides hygiene services to the food industry and had been there for close to twenty years. This company really cared about its employees. They celebrated almost every public holiday, everyone's birthday and personal milestones, and they would all show up when any of them had a party at their homes. They were like a family. Anna did not really enjoy her job, but tolerated it in order to be part of this group of people.

Some of you can relate to this scenario, while some will wonder if any fun work environment is enough to compensate for staying in a job you don't like. We can make a case for both, but we must not underestimate the power of the desire to belong (level three in Maslow's hierarchy of needs).

This need for belonging is a universal need; it is innate to humans and many animals. As social beings, we are wired for connection with others starting in the womb, where we are connected by an umbilical cord to our mothers. Once born, this need is amplified. It's a wonder to see how a crying baby responds when they are carried and cuddled. This need for belonging helps shape our identity; we identify with our family, tribe, nation, etc. We cannot overstate the importance of the need to belong.

People who work at Level 3 are driven by the comfort of belonging; they like the people with whom they work, and the culture of the company. This is the sole reason why they come to work every day. To their colleagues, they may be viewed as loyal to the company, and this may be true, but they are really trading their time for a sense of belonging. They often earn enough money to meet their needs and are not focused on survival (Level 1). Their satisfaction is more extrinsic, as they identify with what the company or team stands for, and they derive fulfillment from playing a part in the team's big picture.

The person working at this level may not really enjoy or be satisfied with the work they do, it may be a real struggle for them and they cope by acquiring skills for the job, but they know the job itself is not their ideal choice. But the comfort of belonging is greater than the desire to risk and seek the unknown. They think, *Hey, I have a job and I really like the people I work with.*

How to Move Out of Level 3

Moving out of this level is a battle against your comfort zone. It will not be easy, especially if it will mean leaving the company and people you've enjoyed being around for years. It will feel like separating from family, but it will be worth it in the end. To move from Level 3, start with the steps in Level 2 and add the following.

1. Discover your natural abilities.

I told you I'd mention this a number of times. This step is critical. Use assessments and introspection as discussed in Chapter 3 to help you identify your natural abilities.

2. Take inventory of your skills.

Skills enable us to function better in our jobs; they are acquired (learned and not natural). I believe we should all work in our abilities zone and acquire skills to support and enhance our performance. Most people have never taken the time to think through and list out all the skills they've acquired in their lifetime. Try it. You'll be amazed at what you've learned.

List everything you've learned on the job, and even off the job. With this list, you'll have a good base of experience to draw from when applying for a new position. Organize the skills into work/technical skills and people skills like leadership skills, listening skills, conflict-management skills, and more (which make a huge impact on your value to any organization). This list will give you a good picture of what you have and what you lack. This list is for you, so be candid in your assessment. You may choose to share it with one or two close confidants who can add to what you've listed.

Listing out and matching your relevant skills with your talents will show you that you are more equipped than you think, and this should give you more confidence to step beyond your comfort zone. There is often a boost in self-belief, which helps overcome self-doubt.

3. Look for ideal positions in your company.

This should be the first option for those who like their company. They know and are part of the culture and will have relations internally that may help facilitate their transfer to an ideal role. This is easier for people who work for a large organization, as they offer more opportunities than smaller companies. This should not be a limiting factor. If your company, large or small, does not have an ideal position for you, be open to looking at other organizations. Refresh your résumé based on the ideal combination of strengths and skills, and seek out recruiters or review desirable positions posted on job boards. Also leverage your external network; you'll be amazed at what you can get and learn from the people you know.

In making this transition, some may face the reality of not having enough experience to do what they want. This may mean taking a lower position in order to acquire the relevant experience and skills for the position they want. For some, this can be a hard pill to swallow, but I encourage you to think of the upside—you step back for a period in order to prepare and be equipped to spend the rest of your working life doing what you'll enjoy. Think of this as a slingshot. In order to jump forward, you have to go back. This gives you the momentum you need for the future.

NOTE FOR MANAGERS:

It is important for you to learn how to create an environment that your team members want to be a part of. There are so many business benefits to this, so don't take it for granted. High-performing teams don't just happen; they are built. I have seen situations where close-knit and high-performing teams are destroyed after mergers and acquisitions. Number crunchers and bottom-line thinkers literally squash the goose that's been laying the golden eggs. This creates a loss of morale, which eventually leads to people leaving the organization. Your team members should be treated as your greatest asset. They are.

Level 4: I Work Because I Use My Natural Abilities

Working in Level 4 means you are either in your career sweet spot, or very close to it. This is what most people desire and few achieve; it is where work satisfaction and engagement start. Identifying your natural abilities is critical to working in your career sweet spot because your abilities determine your ideal work types and work environment. If you are lost on what these mean, you are not alone; most people are, and this is the problem. Let me briefly explain both terms.

Work Types: According to the Highlands Company (creator of the Highlands Ability Battery), these are the translation of your natural abilities into roles and responsibilities that are typical in just about any occupation. Work Types are functions, not jobs. And every job will consist of multiple functions carried out on a regular basis. For example, a manager may be required to set direction, plan work schedules, sell, coach others, solve technical problems, research solutions, present to clients or senior leadership, brainstorm new ideas, etc. Each role (function) constitutes a Work Type, and each Work Type uses one or more abilities. The ideal job is one in which you spend much of your time working in your ideal Work Types.

Work Environment: This refers to the context or environment that is most conducive to your performing at your best (Highlands description). Factors to consider include the pace of work, the amount of teamwork required, the amount of people interaction involved, and the degree of structure within which work is done. Your natural abilities determine the environment in which you'll be most productive.

To learn more about these, please visit the Highlands Company website at www.highlandsco.com.

A good understanding of your natural abilities makes it easier to identify your ideal combination of work types and work environment. In reality, few people will ever have a job with a 100 percent work type/environment match. A perfect match should not be the goal. I encourage my clients to aim for a 65–85 percent match. What matters more is that the job responsibilities tied to your ideal work types are of high value to your team and organization. If you are naturally wired to sell and are good at it, but selling is of little value to your team, it should not be an ideal work type you prioritize in that job.

People who work in Level 4 are driven by a deep sense of value; they know their value and derive satisfaction by giving this value to their organization. They have gotten here by introspection and learning about who they are and how they are. Level 4 workers don't look for a job, they look for a place where they can add value. Work for them is a partnership with their organization; they are not just there to earn a paycheck but to add value and be compensated for that value. They evaluate job offers based on intrinsic factors first and not extrinsic factors like pay or benefits.

People who work in their sweet spot are more creative and more productive than other employees and live a more fulfilled life overall. Their self-knowledge and self-awareness make them very selective in jobs they take on, and they find it easier to turn down offers that do not align with how they are wired.

In the context of working in your career sweet spot, Level 4 is the goal for most people. Unfortunately, many fail to get there. As much of an achievement as getting to this level is, it is still not the highest level of work satisfaction. There is still Level 5.

How to Grow in Level 4

At Level 4 you are working in your sweet spot, and the focus is not transition but growth (increasing your capacity to do more). This is where skill building becomes very important.

Finding your career sweet spot is an exciting thing and something to which everyone should aspire. However, life happens, and things change; this makes it important to learn how to remain in your sweet spot. Here's the key point: staying in your career sweet spot does not mean staying in the same job or at the same company. It means being able to change jobs and still have your ideal work types and environment in place.

Staying in your career sweet spot does not mean staying in the same job or at the same company. It means being able to change jobs and still have your ideal work types and environment in place.

At an executive workshop in 2020, I met a man who had worked as an emergency room nurse and an emergency medical technician (EMT) for close to ten years and loved it. He was now a healthcare administrator and loves it. I initially thought this was an odd move, going from a high-intensity and chaotic work environment to what seemed to be a fairly stable and structured work environment. As I asked him more questions, I realized that both positions had a steady stream of problems which required rapid problem-solving abilities, and this is what he loved about both jobs. Because he knew his strengths and ideal work type and environment, he was able to switch jobs without leaving his career sweet spot.

Staying in your career sweet spot requires two things:
1. A Commitment to growth
2. Deeper self-awareness

1. A Commitment to Growth

Working hard to learn about your strengths and then getting the right job with what you've learned is a process that requires commitment. That said, getting that job in your sweet spot can also become a hindrance to personal and professional growth. Some people may unconsciously go into cruise control as they get accustomed to the new role and all it entails. To avoid that, we must remain actively engaged in getting better at what we do. Looking for ways to improve performance at work should be every employee's personal goal. You don't need to make big leaps, just small, consistent progress. Your progress may not even be immediately noticeable, but over time it will become apparent.

To do this, adopt the strategy used by athletes. They break down their sport into many small parts in order to identify the ones which contribute most to winning. They focus on one part, break it down into smaller parts, then focus on improving on one micro-aspect at a time. In the workplace, we call this skill building: soft skills and technical skills. Soft skills have to do with people interaction, and technical skills relate to technical knowledge of the job you do.

Break down your work into its smallest parts, rank them in order of highest priority, and then, starting with the highest-priority task, identify a few things you can do to improve how you execute that task. Then select one thing to work on and focus on that one thing until you make the improvement you want. Then move on to something else.

This will take intentional effort, and you may be tempted to think, *I'm just too busy.* You are never too busy to get better. Allocate ten to fifteen minutes on a regular basis to getting better.

2. Deepening Your Self-Awareness

This is a form of personal development, but I want to address it as a standalone point. A commitment to personal/professional growth is all about developing oneself, but a commitment to deepening self-awareness is focused on knowing more about oneself. Your present self is a composite of all you've experienced in the past, both good and bad, and there are moments when we unconsciously react to a situation based on triggers from these past experiences.

Take money, for example. The way we think about money is often shaped by the dynamics of the family environment in which we are raised. I've worked with people who were driven to earn more because of a deep fear of lack or an insecurity which stemmed from growing up in a family with little means, and constantly seeing or hearing parents argue over money. Some people may also have a fear of failure or a desire to please others even if it is to their detriment. To their coworkers, these people may be seen as driven and hardworking, but their motivation comes from a very unhealthy place. Like a slightly corrupted operating system, many people have some negative scripts running in their subconscious, which is like our human operating system, resulting in unhealthy motivations to thought patterns which may impede progress in life.

Deepening your self-awareness means learning to pay more attention to your thoughts and actions to identify behavior and thought patterns that may be an obstacle to fully living and growing in your career sweet spot. I once coached a guy who grew up in a family with parents who used guilt trips and constant comparison as tools for motivating their kids to excel. He was a compliant child and wanted to please his parents. Excel he did, but the negative consequence was never feeling good enough and constantly comparing himself to others. This carried over into his adult life. At work, he would take on more projects than he could handle and would put undue pressure on himself to meet an expectation which he perceived had been set by his boss, but in reality was just out of a desire to please the boss. When he found his career sweet spot based on his strengths, this inner battle would have sabotaged him if left unaddressed. He sought the help of a therapist to get to the root of his problem.

If the thought of seeing a therapist makes you uncomfortable, think about the cost of living with deep unresolved issues which may hinder your performance. There are many issues for which working with a trained expert will be better, faster, and cheaper in the long run. Unfortunately, there are still cultures that shun any form of counseling or therapy to their detriment.

The good news is that most of the inner issues you uncover will not need therapy. Simply being aware of a wrong thought pattern will help you manage yourself better as you work through the process of changing the thought pattern. I have had to work through a number of these bad thought patterns as well. One example is how I related to money. After I got married, I realized that my wife and I often argued about money. I would tense up when she talked about buying anything or going window-shopping. Sorry, but if we aren't buying windows, there is no need to go shopping for them. She just found it relaxing to browse through clothing and furniture stores. I, on the other hand, lived in fear that we didn't have enough money, even though we did. It was maybe after four or five years into our marriage that I started exploring why I would tense up whenever my wife and anyone else would ask for money. I soon realized I was reenacting what I saw growing up. My dad was a mechanical engineer and a senior executive at the Nigerian Railway Corporation, meaning we had an upper-middle-class lifestyle. I am not sure why, but anytime I'd ask for money to do anything, my dad's first response would be, "Where do you expect me to get the money?" Ninety percent of the time, he would give me the money to get what I needed, but he always started with this question. Maybe it was his way of ensuring I didn't take the comforts we had for granted. The outcome for me was an unconscious sense of lack even when there was more than enough. Once I identified this as the root problem, I learned to address and soothe my tension when money was discussed, and stopped thinking my wife was just a spendthrift, which she wasn't (turns out I'm actually the bigger spender in our marriage).

The things that trip us up may be certain types of people, situations, expectations, etc. Become a student of yourself; identify your negative scripts and do the work to correct or eliminate them. You'll be better for it.

Know When It's Time to Change Jobs

Times change, things change, we change—and often. So does the workplace. There are times we leave a company because the workplace has changed, and there are times we leave because we have changed.

When the Workplace Changes

This can happen for many reasons: your company acquires, or is acquired by, another company; you get a new boss or are assigned to a new team; corporate priorities may shift. There are many other reasons which are not in your control. Any of these can throw your sweet spot out of balance: the environment may become more chaotic or isolated; an acquiring company may want you to follow a new structure; tasks aligned with your natural abilities may be replaced with those more aligned with your skills (not natural abilities).

When you are out of your sweet spot, you'll know. The change may be sudden or subtly imposed over time. Either way, at some point you will feel a dissonance within you. At this point, you should critically assess the situation and determine if the change is temporary, tolerable, or toast, temporary meaning it's for a short period and you are willing to wait for things to return to normal, tolerable meaning it's permanent but you still have enough elements of your sweet spot and you adapt to the change, and toast meaning the change is permanent and you have no sweet spot elements in use. If the situation is toast, there are two options: stay or leave. Staying means accepting a suboptimal work environment (it may or may not be toxic), which will kick you back into Sunday blues/Friday highs, and leaving means finding another ideal opportunity to add value. I say leave, but not immediately. If it's possible to look for another job while in your current position, do so. If it's not, then develop a transition plan: cut personal expenses, make sure you have enough savings to see you through at least six months, then leave. When you leave, don't take a holiday. Make finding your next opportunity a full-time job. When you find the position, ask for a start date that will give you some time to rest and recharge.

When You Change

As you acquire experience and develop personally and professionally, there should come a time when you outgrow your position and are ready to move to a new one. This should mean a promotion, either at your current company or taking a new position at a different company. Moving up the corporate ladder is a good thing if you are moving in your sweet spot. This said, there are some people for whom a promotion is not their desire. They have found their sweet spot; they love it and they add immense value to the organization. A promotion would mean they get to do less of the work they love and are good at, and more administrative and management work, which they may not enjoy. This would obviously be a morale and productivity killer. Such high-value employees should be allowed to stay in their current role, but still be given an increase in compensation and benefits. Smart organizations should recognize these types of employees and create an alternative compensation plan in which they can get an increase in compensation and benefits in the role without a promotion. If they've been in a role for long enough, it should be okay for some of these people to earn more than their boss.

For those who do have a desire to move up the corporate ladder, it is important to take control of your growth. You do so by working yourself out of your position and knowing when you've outgrown your position. You outgrow your current position by knowing all there is to know about the position and developing one to three other people to take your place. When your team can function effectively without you, you've outgrown the position.

A few years ago, I was invited to speak to a group of almost one hundred regional managers from a well-known nonprofit organization with offices all over the United States. The topic was on growing in your sweet spot. They were all engaged and enjoying the session, until I started talking about outgrowing your position by developing others to replace you. From their reaction, I knew I had hit a sensitive topic. Since it was not a large audience, I let them know I sensed the resistance in the room and wanted to know why. This became quite the interactive session. The common thread in all the answers I heard was a fear of losing their job if they trained others to replace them. They looked at the same situation I was recommending through the lens of fear instead of through the lens of value. They were more interested in holding on to their position than adding their full value to the organization. It is not an unfounded fear, as there are some low-integrity bosses who look for ways to get employees to do more with lower pay. This was not the case at their company. No one had ever talked to them about working themselves out of their job as a way to move up. They were following the "work-hard-till-you-are-noticed-and-promoted" path. This is not the best strategy for growth, and I helped them understand why—you are giving more control of your career to someone else who may not see the value in what you are doing. But when you master your job, do it well, and train others to do it well, you increase the capacity of the team and will (or should) be seen as a person who does excellent work in their sweet spot and also increases the capacity and productivity of any team they run. I won them over to my way of thinking.

How to Work Your Transition Plan: The Wisdom of Baby Steps

At whatever level you find yourself today, you will need a plan to achieve your desired goal. Some of my clients implemented the outcome of our coaching process and saw results within a few months to a little over a year. Some started the process, got sidetracked, and gave up. One client called me eighteen months after I had worked with him, asking for help with transitioning. I was puzzled because he had created a plan during our session. I soon realized that not only had he not implemented the plan, but he had also forgotten all he learned about his natural abilities. I asked him to take a few weeks to review his assessment reports and the plan we had developed. If, after that, he still needed my help, I'd be happy to work with him again. He called me two months later. He had gone back to working on his original plan and had been offered a position at a company.

The plan works when you work it, and it often requires taking consistent baby steps. I use this analogy because if you've ever seen a child learning to walk, there are a few things you'll notice from which we can learn a lot.

1. They take one step at a time.

Babies are not in a hurry. They yield to their natural schedule. They crawl, then learn to stand, and then try to take their first step. This first step is wobbly and will be for a while. Soon, they can take two steps and then three. But they don't stop taking the steps.

As adults, the lesson for us is to implement our plan in baby steps. Focus on step one, achieve it, and then move to step two. Don't rush your plan, as this may end up discouraging you. Also, taking small actions toward your goal will be more manageable.

2. They get up after they fall.

I've never heard a child cry when they fall while learning to walk.

They either fall on their bum or on their hands and knees, look around, get up, and try again. After a few falls, they resort to crawling for a while, but they soon get up and try to walk again. I've seen babies giggle when they fall on their bum.

As adults, we should not let the fear of making a mistake stop us from moving forward. I recommend that my clients assume that they will make some mistakes and face some rejection as they work their transition plan. This is a normal part of life, and we should accept it as a passing phase and learn from the mistake or failure. But we get up and we take the next step.

3. They hold on to something as they learn.

As babies walk, fall, and get up, they soon learn to walk while holding on to the side of a table, couch, or hand of an adult. They are walking with assistance. They walk a bit on their own and then hold on to something. At this point, they are walking more and falling less.

The lesson here for us is that we need to ask for help. This is not a sign of weakness but really a sign of confidence. It is accepting that you don't know it all or have all the answers, and that you can learn from others. You can get a mentor, pay for a coach, and be open to ask people around you for help as you work your plan.

Just like babies who enjoy the freedom of dashing around the house after they learn to walk, you will enjoy the feeling of achieving your goal and getting into that ideal job/career.

Level 5: I Work Because This Is My Calling

This is what I believe to be the highest level at which we can work. At Level 5, you are living and working in your purpose. This level is so important that it deserves a chapter in this book. The next section and chapter will focus on working in your purpose.

RECAP:

There are five levels of work satisfaction:

1. I work because I need a job.
2. I work because I make more.
3. I work because I like my organization.
4. I work because I use my abilities.
5. I work because this is my calling.

Chapter Six Exercise

1. With what you now know about the levels of work satisfaction, how would you answer the question "Why do you work?"

_____

_____

_____

2. At what level would you say you are now? Are you happy with being here?

_____

_____

_____

3. If you are not happy where you are, what step will you take NOW to start moving toward a better level?

_____

_____

_____

_____

_____

In your journal, start drafting your transition plan. Don't start the next chapter till you've written a few steps you can take to start your transition. Remember, it's a draft and you can tweak this as you go.

_____

_____

_____

_____

_____

_____

_____

_____

_____

_____

_____

WORK IN YOUR PURPOSE

When Your 9-5 Is Your Calling

Is your work a job, a career or a calling?

As a result of complications from diabetes, Dick had his right leg amputated just below the knee yesterday. As I thought about how this would alter Dick's life, I felt sad for him. Dr. Dick Wynn had hired me as an intern at Equip, and quickly became my mentor. This man was always on the go and loved what he did.

How will he handle losing a leg? I wondered. *Will he get frustrated, depressed, or angry at God?* All these thoughts raced through my mind as my wife, Lucy, and I approached the door to his hospital room. I had prepared myself mentally to encourage Dick and his wife, Janet, and to be as positive and uplifting as appropriate. I was in for a big surprise.

I took a deep breath, knocked on the door, opened it, and walked in ever so gently. I saw Dick and stopped dead in my tracks. I looked at Dick, then looked at Janet, who was seated next to his bed. I'm not sure what expression I had on my face, but Janet shrugged her shoulders and gave me the "you-know-Dick" look. I guess I was about to learn more about him.

Dick was sitting up in bed, working on his laptop. He wasn't playing solitaire. He was working. He had his usual childlike spark in his eyes when he was working on something exciting. Seeing the look on my face, he started chuckling and happily added that he was on a work conference call that morning. For a quick second I wondered if they had given him a higher dose of morphine.

How can you lose a leg yesterday, and be thinking about, and actually jumping into, work the next day? Who does that? People like Dick Wynn. People for whom their work is their calling. And they are in every kind of job in every industry.

This incident happened over sixteen years ago, but the impact never left me. During that visit, Dick spent more time encouraging and cheering me up than I did him, and I was the one visiting the patient.

Dr. Dick Wynn was a natural strategic and big-picture thinker who loved to build teams and organizations from scratch, and loved mentoring young people.

His career started in 1962 when he joined Youth for Christ, a Christian organization working with young people around the world. In 1985 Dick was appointed CEO of the organization, and six months later elected as national president of YFC. He served in this capacity till 1991, and in his tenure, launched many new initiatives for the organization that focused on middle school ministry, their national evangelism training conferences, and the relocation of the national headquarters to Colorado. From 1991 to 1996, he moved to Singapore serving Youth for Christ International as Asia-Pacific area director. In 2001, he left YFC and joined Equip, a leadership development organization, where he served as vice president, Emerging Young Leaders. Two years later, Dick went to work for Crown Financial ministries as international vice president to help people develop financial freedom, planning their future and increasing their giving for the purpose of funding the Great Commission.

His first amputation happened in 2004 while he was with Crown Financial Ministries. He zipped through rehab faster than expected, learned to use his prosthetic leg, and was back to his regular work schedule in a very short time. Dick went into semi-retirement in 2006 and moved to Orlando, Florida, to serve as chief of staff at Northlands Church.

In April of 2010, Dick's second leg was amputated. Did that stop him? Heck no! He had a calling to fulfill and quickly learned how to use the new prosthetic leg. An October 2010 event in Bangladesh had been on his calendar and he had no plans of canceling the work trip. He attended the event as planned. Not too long after, he became executive director for a young organization called Care for Pastors. They needed someone who could build an organization from scratch and lay a solid foundation for the future. When he took this job, he was seventy years old. Dick wanted to make an impact on as many people as he could in the world and traveled to seventy-five countries for ministry work in his lifetime.

When your work is your calling, you live with a deeper sense of mission. And you never really stop working. You may slow down a bit due to aging, but you never stop. This is the power of working in your calling.

A Job, Career, or Calling

This book is about helping people live out their purpose through the work they do, their 9–5, their vocation. Call it what you want, I'm talking work. Not volunteering or a hobby. Work, from which you earn your income, either as an employee or employer. My focus is on people in the workforce.

Work takes on a much deeper meaning when it is seen as a calling— *"a strong inner inclination to pursue a certain vocation."* People relate more to this term "calling" when it's used in reference to an inner inclination to become a pastor, missionary, or some other type of religious vocation. This is a correct use of the term, but it also encompasses every type of vocation. It can be a strong inner inclination to be a doctor, soldier, pilot, accountant, dancer, actor, surgeon, dentist, entrepreneur, etc.

Having a strong inner inclination can drive people to good and bad things. It is important to clearly state that in this book I am focused on positive inner inclinations toward a specific legitimate vocation. A strong inner inclination to rob a bank is not a calling; it's an indication to seek mental help.

A calling is not measured by fame, status, or wealth, but by positive impact. There are many famous people who really haven't had a positive impact on their fans. They may be idolized by their fans for their craft, without really adding any positive value or lessons to their lives.

Let's examine what work is like when it is a job, a career, or a calling.

When work is just a job, it is a means to an end, a source of income. When work is just a job, morale and loyalty are often low, and commitment to your employer or organization is low or nonexistent. People for whom work is a job are always on the hunt for a better job opportunity. They are like the person at a party having a conversation with someone but constantly looking around to see who else they can talk with. They are not fully present and engaged where they are and live with the constant sense that the grass is greener elsewhere. They switch employers whenever they can to a seemingly better income-earning opportunity.

When work is a career, the focus is on personal achievement based on growth and upward movement in a particular field. Work as a career will be more fulfilling than work as a job. People here see a longer path in their chosen field and current organization. Their commitment level is higher, as they see a direct connection between the effort they put in and the outcome or gain they expect—a promotion, pay increase, and other benefits.

Being career focused does not always translate to loving what you do and feeling the deep satisfaction that you are giving your gift to society; you may not have that sense of certainty that this is what you are meant to do with your life.

When work is a calling, there is a sort of divine aspect to it. You may have that "Ethan Hunt" feeling from the movie *Mission Impossible*; you've been given a mission and you've accepted the mission (cue music minus the explosion). You have a higher purpose in the work you do, whether you are a janitor, pilot, or chief executive officer, and it shows in how you do your work. You give to the world what you were born to give. You are the right puzzle piece in the right place within this grand puzzle of life.

When your work is a calling, you live with a sense that you have been assigned a specific purpose by your Creator, and your satisfaction and fulfillment are tied to your obedience to this call. In essence, you can't see yourself doing anything else but what you've been assigned to do in that time.

My mentor, Dick Wynn, died unexpectedly in March of 2011 at the young age of seventy-one. I say young because he would have kept going strong into his nineties if he could. The weekend before his death, he conducted a leadership training session for Youth for Christ in Grand Rapids, Michigan. His work was his calling, and he never quit. He loved what he did.

I accept that not everyone will share my views here, and that is okay. I write, speak, and teach with my Christian faith as my foundation, and am focused on fulfilling my purpose, which is *helping people live out their purpose through the work they do.*

The use of the term "calling" means that there is a caller, and a required response. People who see their work as a calling live with a belief that they are responsible to a higher power (the Caller) and with an awareness of eternity and the brevity of time, their time on earth. They are aware they won't live forever and want to play their part in the bigger picture of life. For most of these people, their faith is deeply important to them and their work is not separate from their faith.

This element of faith and working in response to a higher calling is the main difference between working in Level 4 (working in your sweet spot) and working in Level 5 (working in your purpose/calling).

People working in both levels will be in their sweet spot based on their strengths. At Level 4 they will make self-directed decisions based on their strengths, and at Level 5 they make work decisions based on a sense of guidance and direction from God.

RECAP:

Your work can be a job, a career, or a calling:

1. When work is just a job, it is a means to an end, a source of income.
2. When work is a career, the focus is on personal achievement based on growth and upward movement in a particular field.
3. When work is a calling, you live with a sense that you have been assigned a specific purpose by your Creator.

Chapter Seven Exercise

1. Is your current work a job, a career, or a calling?

_____

_____

_____

_____

2. Do you know anyone who considers their work a calling? If yes, write down all the things you like about their view of life and work.

_____

_____

_____

_____

3. Select two or three people whom you know love their work. Call or email them; ask them if they consider their work a career or calling and why. This exercise will give you more insight into the deep satisfaction people get from doing work they love. This will keep you motivated.

3 Ways We Engage Purpose at Work

Always seek to know why!

We've talked about purpose and we've talked about work. Now let's explore living out your purpose through the work you do.

Work is a natural and integral part of life. Nature is constantly at work, evidenced by all the growth and changes observed in plants and animals. Work denotes effort, and effort is expended as growth happens in living organisms—seedlings push through the earth to emerge, babies are pushed out of the womb or egg in order to start their independent life, cells grow and replenish as we grow physically, etc. Your body is working when you are awake and asleep; you can't get away from work. It is a natural process.

Every man-made item was brought to fruition because various people worked to take it from an idea into production, to sales, and then deliver it to the end user. Stop reading for a minute, and just look at the things around you. Imagine all the jobs that were created in the process of developing these items and getting them to your home or office. Each job represents someone's work. We were created to work, and to work in a specific way based on how we are naturally wired. *You are HOW you are for WHY you are.*

We should make it our goal to live out our purpose through the work we do. If your purpose is to teach, teach. If it is to sing, sing. If it's to build, build. Everyone and everything were created for a purpose. Whatever your purpose is, discover it and work in it.

3 Ways We Engage Purpose at Work

In some ways, these will remind you of the 5 Levels of Work Satisfaction in Chapter Six. The content is similar, but I'm now focused on being "purpose-centered" and driving toward living out your life purpose through your job.

1. Self-driven purpose: You work WITH a purpose.
2. Cause-driven purpose: You work FOR a purpose.
3. Divine purpose: You work IN YOUR purpose.

Self-Driven Purpose

When you work with a self-driven purpose, you are driven and motivated by goals and rewards you set for yourself. For example, making a certain volume of sales because of the commission check you'll get, or working on a graduate degree in order to move into a higher-paying job or your desired job/field. Your abilities may or may not be engaged when you work with a purpose; the reward is the chief driver. If you do get to use your abilities, that's great; you'll enjoy what you do. If they are not engaged, your work will not be fun, but you hunker down and push through in order to achieve the reward of your goals. When the goal is achieved, an empty or lost feeling may set in if there is nothing else to aim for. Some people overcome this by constantly setting new goals.

It is not bad to work with a purpose. It definitely keeps one focused and committed to what they are pursuing. If you are in your sweet spot, you use your strengths and abilities to pursue career growth and income goals. Since you are primarily self-directed, you may or may not care about the mission or vision of your organization, and you may find it easier to prioritize your goals ahead of the goals of your organization.

The key here is that you do what you do primarily for YOU. Your goals and drivers are YOU focused and YOU centered.

This reminds me of Craig, who was chief technology officer (CTO) for a midsize consulting firm. He had worked his way up the corporate ladder with the goal of becoming a CTO and earning the coveted title of CTO of the Year, which is a big deal amongst his peers. I don't know why Craig set his sights on CTO, but he did, and put in a lot of effort to achieve it. He worked long hours and weekends, was okay with as much travel as his company would throw at him, and did whatever it took. He eventually achieved his goal of becoming CTO and earning the coveted CTO of the Year award. Not long after he achieved his goal, I learned he started drinking a little more and ended up having an affair with a lady at work. Could there have been issues in his marriage while he was working on getting to the CTO position? Maybe. But his goals kept him focused. Once the goals were attained, it seemed like he lost focus or direction and went down a bad trail, which caused pain to so many people. His self-directed purpose kept him focused on his target. But once attained, without another strong target, it was easy to lose focus.

Cause-Driven Purpose

The person who works for a cause-driven purpose is driven by something bigger than self. They work for a cause or purpose which stems from their personal life vision or the mission or purpose of their organization. They see themselves as part of a bigger team doing something that makes a positive impact on society. The mission may not mean much to others, but it does to this person, and that's what matters.

THE ELECTRICAL ENGINEER TURNED ADULT DAY CARE PROVIDER

"How the heck do you go from a twenty-plus-year career as an electrical engineer in the telecoms space to running a daycare service for seniors?" I asked. I hadn't seen Poonam in almost five years, and at that time, she was a senior project manager at Ericsson. I was happy to hear she now worked for herself but was really curious about why she chose a senior care business.

"I was doing quite well financially in my engineering career but never felt fulfilled in it. Looking back, I realized I went into engineering because my dad wanted me to be a teacher while he wanted my brother to be an engineer. What? If my brother could do it, so could I. My dad gave his support and that's how my electrical engineering career began. I hunkered down and gave it my all. I knew I wasn't fulfilled, but hey, I had started down this path. I promised myself I'd stay in engineering till age fifty when my kids would be done with school and working, and then I'd go do what would bring fulfillment. I had started thinking about what I really wanted to do back in 2013, and your book *Finding Your Sweet Spot* played a key role in my decision to work with seniors. Going through the exercise in the book where you ask the reader to think back to what they loved to do as a child revealed how while growing up in India, I loved to visit and take care of an older auntie who lived alone. I always felt deep joy when caring for her. The more I thought about this, the more excited and joyful I felt; I knew this was what I wanted to do for the rest of my life and had to figure out an ideal format for serving seniors here in Atlanta. I quit my job in 2015 and started doing the research and planning for what type of senior service I'd offer."

Seva Adult Day Care was founded in 2017 with a vision to create a happy and healthy community which promotes the physical and mental health of seniors with engaging activities and nutritious meals.

Poonam is a good example of someone working for a purpose. She and her team work for the bigger purpose of serving and loving on seniors. Not surprising, the business quickly became profitable and their client base has been growing steadily.

People who are driven by a personal vision are often very clear on their core values and have developed a personal mission from these values. In many ways, they are like the person who works in their purpose; their satisfaction comes from making an impact on others. The source of the purpose is the key difference between a person working for a purpose and the one working in their purpose. When you work for a purpose, the bigger picture or reason comes from you or from your organization. When you work in your purpose, God is the source of your purpose. I know people who have chosen to make the earth cleaner, or ensure that people have access to clean water, or want to develop user-friendly technology, or figure out how to make safer antibacterial medications. These people are not motivated by money, status, fame, etc., only their vision. Their sense of meaning comes from the purpose for which they live. Take it away and they become like a ship without a rudder. This is one of the downsides of working for a purpose.

I am often asked if it's possible that working in your purpose (God-centered) can start from working with a purpose. The answer is yes. You start off using your gifts and abilities for self, or a reason bigger than self, and then hit a turning point where you realize that the work you've been doing is what God wants you to do, and you start focusing on how he wants you to do the work.

Purpose-Driven Corporations

All business entities are started to meet a need, by providing a service or product for a profit. Their primary purpose is not to create jobs or other altruistic purposes. That said, some companies do want to make a positive difference in their space and are driven by this desire. They have such a compelling and engaging vision that employees feel a deep sense of pride and mission working there.

As a coach, I get to work with employees at different organizations. Employees who buy into the mission of their organization always stand out. They see themselves more as custodians and protectors of the organization's mission, and their satisfaction comes from playing a part in helping to achieve it.

LIFE AT JACKSON HEALTHCARE

Jackson Healthcare, headquartered in Alpharetta, Georgia, is one of the largest staffing companies in the United States. It earned *Atlanta Business Chronicle's* "Best Place to Work, Extra-Large Employer" in 2014, 2015, and 2016, and was certified a *"Great Place to Work"* in 2017 and 2018.

My first interaction with them was in 2017 when a company I work for was hired to conduct executive communication coaching workshops for their high-potential employees going through a three-month leadership-development program. On my first day there, I saw a prominently displayed sign that read, ***"We exist to improve the lives of our associates."*** Whenever I hear such statements from an organization, I pay particular attention to see if they live up to it. They sure did. The mission of the company is *"to improve the delivery of patient care and the lives of everyone we touch,"* and the owners were smart enough to boldly proclaim their commitment to their associates. The company invested heavily in a beautiful work environment—cafeteria, gym, and elaborately decorating the campus for the holidays. They created a family-friendly culture (with bring-your-kids-to-work days and a daycare facility) and pursued serious investment in the professional development of employees.

They are not a perfect company but are working hard in the pursuit of their mission. Every Jackson Healthcare employee with whom I've worked loves the company and its culture, and they love coming to work every day. When a company's cause is compelling and they work hard at living their cause, employees have a sense of mission when they come to work.

Most mission-driven organizations tend to treat their employees well. Note, I said most. There are many companies that aren't truly mission-driven and that do not treat their employees well. When my clients ask me how to respond to a toxic work environment, I always respond with the same answer: "Quit." No matter how compelling a mission is, it is not worth enduring a toxic work environment. It is sad when companies with a really good product or service are poorly run. Employees who stay will quickly lose sight of the mission and simply stay on for the paycheck until they find a better alternative. Fortunately, most companies with a compelling mission also have leadership who want to treat their employees well.

I can't understand why some organizations tout their commitment to customer service but treat their employees like crap. Duh! Unhappy employees take their frustration out on customers at some point; it'll show in their work. If you consistently experience poor service from a company, that's a sign that they don't treat employees well.

"Customer first" may sound like a good business strategy, and it's often meant to appeal to customers, but I personally think it's patronizing. I get excited when I see a company that believes in taking care of its employees first. Take good care of them, and they will transfer that care to your customers. Think Disney and Ritz Carlton; here are two companies that have created training programs which other companies emulate.

I've discussed two of the three ways we can engage purpose at work, by working with a purpose and working for a purpose. The third way, working *in* your purpose, will be discussed as a stand-alone chapter next. Yes, it is that important.

Work in Your DIVINE Purpose

I've discussed two of the three ways we engage purpose at work, self-driven and cause-driven purpose. The third way, working in your divine purpose, will be discussed as a stand-alone chapter next. Yes, it is that important.

RECAP:

3 Ways We Engage Purpose at Work:
1. Self-driven purpose: You work WITH a purpose.
2. Cause-driven purpose: You work FOR a purpose.
3. Divine purpose: You work IN YOUR purpose.

Chapter Eight Exercise

1. Think about your current job. Do any of the three ways of engaging purpose apply to you? Think about your last job if currently unemployed.

_____

_____

_____

2. What steps led you to your current work? You needed a job, you were promoted, you were asked to lead a new team, etc. If you don't write out how you got here, you may find yourself here again in a few years. Think deeply and journal your thoughts.

_____

_____

_____

3. Does your organization have a purpose statement? Write it out if you know it.

_____

_____

_____

4. If yes, how is it lived out by company employees?

_____

_____

_____

Work in Your Divine Purpose

Every day of my life was recorded in your book.
Every moment was laid out BEFORE a single day had passed.
~ Psalm 139:16 (NLT)

My core belief, if you haven't figured it out by now, is that each person is created by God for a specific purpose. He is The One who assigns a purpose to each life. Some may refer to this as a calling. I believe that no birth is an accident, no matter the circumstances that led to conception and birth. You are not an accident. It doesn't matter if you were born in a palace or under a bridge to a homeless drug addict; God's fingerprint on you is unique, and no else has that print.

Where you were born cannot hinder the fulfillment of your purpose. Heck, let me say that again. *Where you were born cannot hinder the fulfillment of your purpose.* Only you have the power to do that.

You were born at a certain time and place and into a specific family for a reason. God has given us the complete freedom and free will to choose what we do and how we live. We can choose what He has planned for our life, or we can chart our own course and live out what we choose. The choice is ours.

Being committed to discover and to live out your purpose is the key to fulfillment and deep satisfaction in life.

Being committed to discover and live out your divine purpose is the key to fulfillment and deep satisfaction in life. No need to wonder if your life matters or makes a difference; you will be so busy fulfilling your purpose, questions like that won't arise. The sense of certainty and direction gives your life a passionate focus. Even when you slack off for one reason or another, you know where to pick right up and keep forging forward.

For those who may not share my belief in God, you will find satisfaction and fulfillment working in Level 4, your career sweet spot. These people know their natural abilities and how and where best to engage them. You will be of immense value to our world if you achieve this. And you can choose to stop reading this book at this point. If you are curious, though, to learn what working in your purpose looks like, then read on.

The God Factor

To work *in* your divine purpose, I believe you must have a belief in, and a relationship with, God. It is unfortunate that many people want to separate God from work; they say the secular should be separated from the spiritual. When you examine this in depth, you'll realize how absurd it is. If you believe that you were created by God, then you'll also understand that He created you with certain abilities for a reason.

As we've established earlier, work is a gift—a blessing—especially when we work as He intended. My goal is to help the reader start the process of discovering their divine purpose and then focus on working in that purpose. Your purpose is central to your life; you are here to contribute something. Your purpose is not a hobby; purpose is a vocation. Your purpose is not something you do for fun in your spare time, purpose should consume you and direct your career path. Purpose is work. Will you have fun in your purpose? Yes, but it'll have its share of challenges. And the challenges will not stop you. Life is full of good and tough times; that's just the reality. Living in your purpose will not change that. You are, however, encouraged by the fact that you are moving in the right direction and doing what you were born to do.

Working in your divine purpose combines the earlier definitions of work and purpose.

> **Work: to tend and care in order to create and multiply**
> **Purpose: the reason for the existence of something**
>
> Working in your purpose means that you *attend to and care for the reason for which you were created in order to bring increase and develop something new.*

When you work in your sweet spot, you use your abilities to serve others. When you work in your divine purpose, you use your abilities to serve God by serving people. The difference is in who comes first, God or you. I say this because there are many successful people who have built great businesses and are very philanthropic. And this is good. But some don't believe in God, and trust more in their efforts and what they've achieved. The person working in their divine purpose, whether to build a multibillion-dollar company or to teach math to kids in elementary school, works with a sense of being on a mission from God. They give their full attention to their work in order to first, serve and please God, and second, to serve people.

Working in your purpose means that you *attend to and care for the reason for which you were created in order to bring increase and develop something new.*

God loves increase. This truth is both a natural and spiritual law. Every living thing grows; the first words spoken to man in Genesis 1:28 were, "Be fruitful, multiply, replenish, sub-

> **Working in your purpose means that you attend to and care for the reason for which you were created in order to bring increase and develop something new.**

due, and have dominion." If you can wrap your mind and heart around this, you will see and appreciate that God has an amazing plan for every person He's created. I won't go deep into the spiritual discourse on this verse, but I need to touch briefly on the third word, "replenish." To replenish means "to make full or complete AGAIN, as by supplying what has been used up." The five words from "be fruitful" to "have dominion" take on a deeper meaning when you grasp the importance of the middle word "replenish."

Before there is a replenishing, there first has to be a depletion. Nothing created in the physical world is meant to be permanent. Living things grow old and eventually die—depletion. In the work world, knowledge, ideas, technology, processes, etc. become outdated and irrelevant (depleted) and in need of an update or upgrade.

Twenty years ago, self-driving cars were found only in movies. Today, there are many companies working on the technology for self-driving cars. Twenty years from now, we may just be wondering how we survived without self-driving cars. You see this change and growth in different industries. Updates are automatically made to the apps on your phone frequently, as the developers never stop thinking of ways to improve their performance. Do you remember when you had to wait months or even a year for new updates to software we used? And we often had to pay for those updates. Most companies today send out software updates (replenish) frequently without cost if they want to remain relevant to their users.

This word, "replenish," and its meaning are critical to our understanding of the importance of our purpose. You are created for a certain purpose, at a certain time in a certain place. We each play a part in the replenishment of outdated ideas, processes, products, etc. The enhancements to the apps we use come from people thinking and working on ways to make them better.

The progression from fruitfulness to dominion can be seen as a constant cycle, and one which gives every person alive the opportunity to play an active and unique role if they choose to accept their purpose.

The Cycle of Increase

Fruitfulness

Fruits start with a seed. Plant and nurture the seed and it will mature to a point where it starts to produce fruit of its kind. An apple seed will grow into an apple tree and produce apple fruit. You will never see guava fruit or watermelons coming from an apple seed or tree.

I liken this to a person who identifies their purpose. As there are different kinds of seeds, so also are there diverse purposes for human beings to fulfill. After discovering your purpose and abilities, you nurture them to a point where they can be lived out through the work you do. Unlike plant seeds that follow their natural course, humans have the free will to pursue any path they desire. The unfortunate result of this is that many people are unconsciously living and working as lemons when they really are a pineapple or avocado.

When you discover your purpose, this cycle really plays out in your work life as an employee or entrepreneur. Using your abilities in the right environment, you can become very productive in the work you do. You become fruitful because you have developed your abilities and know how to use them.

Multiply

The seeds in the fruit from a single tree, if replanted, can quickly become an orchard. In the context of working in your purpose, you go from being productive alone to helping others become productive. This is exponential growth through developing others, growing your team, expanding the influence of your work or business or idea. You multiply by becoming very good at what you do, and others outside your immediate work community start to seek your expertise.

Replenish

We need new fruit because we've either eaten what we have, or they've become rotten. Thank God for this aspect of renewal in nature.

In the context of your purpose, this is where things really change. As your expertise and productivity increase, you will start to develop new ways of doing things, making improvements and enhancements to what already exists, and even inventing new things. Creativity kicks in here, and new ideas are birthed. Growth through fruitfulness and multiplication brings you to a point where you should have something new to add to the world.

Subdue

To subdue connotes tension, a resistance to the new thing you have to give. This is the point where the old clashes with the new; new ideas, processes, thinking, products, etc. start to challenge the status quo. Mankind has made progress and evolved in how we do things because of this tension. Once people settle into a pattern of thinking or behaving, making a shift can be a real struggle. I am not sure why, but most of us are initially resistant to change that we didn't initiate. In the context of work, you must be willing to defend your ideas and push hard for them. If the change you suggest is the right thing for the time, it will be adopted or will influence the final product or outcome. If you don't relent, you will overcome the old ways.

Dominate

At this point, the new idea or process is adopted and becomes the in-thing, the flavor of the season. Everyone loves it and accepts it, and it serves its purpose; it has its time on stage. But remember, this is a cycle that never stops, and we are all at different phases in the process. We are growing and creating new ideas and things which, at some point, will challenge our current status quo and eventually replace it. Just think about how mobile phones have changed over the years. I remember when Nokia handsets dominated the market, then Blackberry soon took its place, and after a while came the iPhone. What will come next is the big question, but it is inevitable that something else will, at some point, replace the dominance of the iPhone, and it most likely will not be a brand we know of today.

3 Parts to Working in Your Divine Purpose

Working in your divine purpose means that you "***attend to*** *and care for* ***the reason*** *for which you were created in order to bring* ***increase*** *and develop something new.*"

When you work in your purpose, this cycle never stops. Looking at this cycle, there are three key things that drive it:

1. The Reason (Your Purpose)
2. Your Attention
3. The Increase

The Reason (Your Purpose)

Discovering your divine purpose should trigger a sense of urgency within you. It is your mission, your reason for being, and you go to work on it. In my work as a career coach, I show my clients the impact their natural abilities have on them, whether they are conscious of it or not. We mostly behave in a manner that is consistent with how we are wired. When you become aware of how you are wired, and the reason why you are alive, it starts to impact how you live.

Discovering your divine purpose activates this cycle in your life.

Your Attention

I just said that once you discover your purpose, it starts to factor into how you live your life. But it doesn't take away the other things competing for your attention. The strong pull or call of your purpose will always be present, but your response, the attention you give, is a choice you have to make over and over again. Will you get sidetracked? Yes, often. And when you do, work hard at bringing your focus back to your purpose. Prioritizing and focusing on your purpose is how you nurture and develop yourself and identify where and how best to use your gifts. Attention also keeps you in touch with external changes that can affect how you serve God and others. Attention keeps you dependent on God for guidance; you didn't choose your purpose, so look to Him for direction.

The attention you give to nurturing your abilities and working in your purpose is what leads to the third part, increase.

The Increase

Growth, like I said earlier, is a natural part of life. If you attend to your purpose, growth will naturally occur in your life. And I don't just mean physical growth. Your purpose is meant to add something to the world, something that others will need and use. This is the increase I'm talking about—the outcome and reason for your purpose.

Increase comes from productivity and creativity. The innovative ideas that are birthed by each person add something new to the world. When you work in your purpose, you can't help but be creative; you will either improve on what already exists or come up with something totally new. Hint, if The Creator made us in His Image and Likeness, don't you think He wants to create through us? I believe so.

Benefits of Working in Your Divine Purpose

Confidence

Confidence is a desirable trait, and often quite appealing when we meet a very confident person. Working in your purpose comes with a measure of confidence that will amaze and often confuse others. A person working in their purpose lives with a sense of destiny and will often make decisions based on what they sense is in line with where they are going in life. Their actions may seem odd in the present, and persons themselves may not fully understand. But they know it's the right thing to do. The person who lives for their purpose will seek God's guidance and respond to His direction.

In 1998, I lived in Lagos, Nigeria, and had been running a small landscaping business for almost three years. The early years in my business were tough, but I persisted. By 1998, I had a few corporate clients, had worked on a sizable residential project, and the business seemed like it was finally about to become profitable. In that year, however, I sensed God leading me to move to Zambia as a missionary. It did not make sense to me, but I knew it was what I had to do. My family and friends thought I was making a very bad decision, and that I would regret it. There was little support, with some people making very harsh comments. I must admit, I was afraid of the unknown, but decided to trust God on this issue.

I shut down my business in March of 1998 and moved to Zambia in June of the same year. I lived there for three years, and then moved to America in 2001. While I lived in Nigeria, I never had a desire to move to America. But Zambia changed that; I soon realized that I wanted to explore the world and was open to moving to another country. Soon after I moved to America, I got to work as an intern at leadership guru John Maxwell's company Equip. There I was personally mentored by an amazing leader, Dr. Dick Wynn, who was a vice president at the company. My time there exposed me to resources and leaders who helped me grow as a leader. I did not know who John Maxwell was until I moved to Zambia and began looking for leadership-development resources to help me grow. I love to help people see that there is a purpose to their life and discovered this while working as a pastor in Zambia. I also met my wife in Atlanta. Her sister, who introduced us, had worked with me in Zambia. Looking back, my three years in Zambia marked a major turning point in my life. Without Zambia, I may not be where I am today.

When you make a decision in line with your purpose, no matter the immediate outcome, you can rest assured that it is the right decision. This confidence brings a deep sense of peace and rest, even during turbulent times.

Adventure

This may sound odd as a benefit to working in your purpose, but it really is one. When you go on a journey with The Creator, nothing about your life will be ordinary. There will be experiences and opportunities that others won't have in their lives. Your purpose was chosen by The One who made everything, and you will often find yourself in situations where you'll wonder, *How the heck did I get here?* What may seem impossible to others somehow seems to come through for you because there is a divine part to what you are doing.

The goal is not for you to brag on your experiences, but to be humbled by them. My adventures with God remind me that I'm not in control. Working in your purpose may place you in front of people others feel are "out of reach," give you work with very sharp people, or invite input on some amazing projects. I have an uncle who was a chemistry professor at Clark Atlanta University in Georgia. In his mid-fifties, he felt an inner leading to quit teaching and to start a leadership institute focused on transforming developing nations. Many people wondered if he had lost his mind. I mean, what does chemistry have to do with nation building? Ten years after launching his organization, he has offices in about twelve countries and consults with heads of state in developing nations.

Working in your purpose means working for God. Trust me when I say there is no adventure that can come close to this.

Increased Productivity

When you work in your strength zone, you are much more productive. In your strength zone, you are able to work faster than others, which gives you more capacity, and you are also more creative than others. When you work in your purpose, God gets more involved in what you do. The best way I can describe this is to say that God has more vested in us fulfilling our purpose than we do. It is His world and His plan, and He's assigned each of us a part to play. Each person's part/purpose is connected to and affects the purpose of others. The ultimate winner is God, and trust me, He never loses. When you work in your purpose, your output and influence will often be more than you can achieve on your own. This is better experienced than described.

Deep Fulfillment

When you work in your purpose, there is a sense of fulfillment that comes from knowing you are doing what you were born to do. Why would anyone want to live life as a spectator, or worse, playing the part of another person? When you find your fit, you truly come alive. You live with the sense of giving your part to the world, making your unique imprint on it.

Many people live life in constant comparison with others; we know we shouldn't, but we still do (some more or less than others). Hey, I'm speaking to myself as I write this. It's really foolish to compare, and I try to remind myself of this often. It is easy to unconsciously compare oneself to others—career, income, lifestyle, etc. When we do this, we can never feel good about ourselves, no matter if we think we are doing better than others or that others are doing better than us. We'll never feel good about the comparison. If you think others are doing better than you, you'll feel down. If you feel others are doing worse than you, you may hope they don't become better than you. This is a no-win situation. Knowing and working in your purpose gives you your true north, a sense of direction and accomplishment which comes from playing the part only you were created to play.

Think deeply about this. No one else can take your place and do what you were created to do. No one else has your assignment. It gives me immense joy and fulfillment when I write, speak, or coach people on different topics which help them function better in their purpose. I am a positive enabler. When I go through tough times or experience failure in something, I quickly remind myself of this and it helps me get back on track. I am fulfilled when I help people perform better in their purpose.

RECAP:

Working in your purpose means that you attend to and care for the reason for which you were created in order to bring increase and develop something new.

Working in your divine purpose comes with:

1. A sense of confidence
2. A life of adventure
3. Increased productivity
4. And deep fulfillment

Chapter Nine Exercise

1. Do you believe God created you for a specific purpose?

_____

_____

_____

_____

_____

_____

_____

2. If you answered no to the above question, write the reasons why you don't believe.

_____

_____

_____

_____

_____

_____

_____

3. Looking at the Cycle of Increase—be fruitful, multiply, replenish, subdue, dominion—which are present or missing in your work today?

_____

_____

_____

_____

_____

_____

_____

_____

4. What is holding up the cycle in your life?

_____

_____

_____

_____

_____

_____

5. What will you do to fix this?

_____

_____

_____

_____

_____

_____

CHAPTER TEN

How to Find Work in Your Purpose

S o, how do you actually seek and find employment in your divine purpose? That's what this is all about, correct? Yep. This is where the rubber meets the road and all that we've talked about is put into practice. I interviewed a few friends who are in the corporate world and who identify as working in their purpose. Their stories bring to life what I've written about, and from them we can learn quite a bit.

Playing in the Sandbox

If anyone had told Natalie Born that she would one day derive deep fulfillment by helping leaders and organizations develop and launch new things, she would not have believed them. While earning a business degree, she worked part time at a call center for CareerBuilder to pay for college. She never imagined launching her corporate career there, so it was quite the surprise when she was offered a promotion and full-time position as an account manager within their customer service department.

"I was growing and learning a lot as the company allowed me to try new roles and work on different projects. At some point, my boss, and mentor at the time, encouraged me to build my career in product development

because he believed I could go very far in that space. I kept this in mind, and not too long after our conversation, a product development position opened up. I applied for it and got it. Product development felt like such a natural fit for me, like it was what I was meant to do. Since then, I've used every new position to learn, grow, and stretch myself in the product development and innovation space. Some jobs I enjoyed, and some I disliked, but each one pushed me closer to what I would love. My work feels like I'm playing in a sandbox; I love developing and launching new things."

When I interviewed Natalie, she had been in the workforce for twenty years with five different companies. The first six years were spent in customer service and project management, and the rest in product development, rising from product development manager to SVP business development and then leaving to start her innovation strategy firm Innovation Meets Leadership, which helps companies develop and launch services and products they are passionate about.

Natalie's story is like that of most people I've studied and talked with who are working in their purpose or calling. One key thing I noticed in the lives of these people is that their journey to working in their purpose seemed to go through three phases.

1. Discovery
2. Preparation
3. Fulfillment

These phases will not always manifest in the same manner in each person's life, as God deals with us differently, but I believe this is the path to working in your divine purpose. Let's look at each one.

DISCOVERY: Identify Your Purpose

I want to be clear; I'm not talking about discovering your abilities here. Abilities, personality, and all the forms of self-knowledge discussed in Chapter Three play a part in this journey, but I am isolating the discovery of your purpose in this section. I said it earlier—you cannot separate purpose from The Creator; only the maker of a thing can define the purpose of the thing. The same with your purpose; many things in this journey are tied to God.

There are four steps to discovering your purpose:

1. Belief that you have a purpose
2. Introspection
3. Inner feeling/sensing
4. Praying about it

Belief That You Have a Purpose

This is where it all starts. I find that most people have a subconscious feeling that there is something more to life and a purpose to their existence. We all respond to this inner tug differently. Some press on to search; some ponder the meaning of life endlessly; some, sort of, push it aside and focus on working on what they can see. Then you have the few who choose to believe and live by the mantra "You become what you choose to become."

Have you ever lost your cell phone or car keys? How do you feel when searching for them? Frustrated, I bet. This frustration happens because you know deep down inside that your phone or car keys are somewhere; there is an inner certainty that keeps you looking till you find them. Contrast that with shopping for a pair of jeans that are a perfect fit for you. Hey, we've all searched for jeans at some point. You go from store to store trying on different pairs and hoping to find one that fits. With your lost phone or keys, your search is based on knowing you have them, and it is a very strong feeling. With the jeans, you have a strong wish, hoping to find the right pair.

Believe that you have a purpose, just like you search for your phone or keys with a sense of certainty. Don't look for your purpose with a wishful desire like you do the nice pair of jeans. Here's why: you were created

The longing for meaning and purpose in life is wired into each person; it's almost like our subconscious holds eternal truths but can't do anything until our conscious mind takes the lead.

for a purpose. Believing is first and is a critical part of this process. It's also the step most people struggle with, as they often judge their lives by their current circumstances. Your mistakes, failures, tragedies, successes, or present situation do not determine or influence your purpose.

You were created for a purpose; your subconscious mind knows this. You are not some random gene carrier roaming the earth. The longing for meaning and purpose in life is wired into each person; it's almost like our subconscious holds eternal truths but can't do anything until our conscious mind takes the lead.

If you believe, you will discover your purpose.

Introspection *(refer to Chapter Three for details)*

"Know thyself" is a quote that has been made famous over the centuries, and it drives home, in clear and simple terms, how important it is to know how we are wired. *You are how you are for why you are*; your purpose will be achieved using your gifts and abilities. In my work as a career coach, I use assessments to help my clients get a clearer picture of how they are wired. The more you know about yourself, the closer you are to understanding what you should do with your life. A biblical principle is that God will not give you a purpose for which He hasn't equipped you. Read the Parable of the Talents in Matthew 25. Verse 15 makes a very important statement that is often overlooked:

*"To the one he gave five bags of gold, to another two bags, and to another one bag, **each according to his ability**."*

Each person was given a quantity of gold based on their individual capacity. As my clients learn more about themselves, they feel so much joy from whittling down their ideal career options. Most people are overwhelmed in their career search because they think they have too many options. This comes from the erroneous mindset that says, "You can be anything you want to be." I don't believe we can be anything we want to be, but we can be all we were created to be.

Inner Feeling or Sensing

There are people who have always had a sense or inner feeling about what to do with their lives. I've heard statements like, "I've always had the desire to work with kids," or be a nurse, or be a musician, or sell things, or lead people, etc. The inner sensing or feelings some people have often come from their subconscious, and some respond to the tug while others ignore it. I need to make clear that we all have a subconscious sense that there should be a purpose/meaning to our existence, but not everyone will have the sense of what to do emanate from their subconscious as well. I wish it did for everyone, but it doesn't. And it doesn't really give those who have this sense an advantage; we can all identify our purpose if we choose to.

Sometimes, when people start working on identifying their natural abilities, they may start to feel an inclination or desire to use their strengths in a particular way. It may be that the affirmation/confirmation of our individual abilities awakens the inner sense of what we should do with our gifts.

From when I was a child, I had a sense that there was a purpose to my life, a sense that I would somehow make a positive change in the world. It may have been brushed off as a childish dream, but I never really let go of it. I didn't pursue it either; I just let it sit there. After I gave my life to Jesus in November of 1995, the desire to figure out what that tug was became stronger. I had the inner belief and inner sense but didn't know exactly what to do with it.

Having the inner belief with or without the inner sense of what to do will not give you a clear picture of what you should do. This is where the next step, prayer, becomes critical.

Praying About It

You will notice I keep emphasizing that we are the created and not The Creator. The Creator made you for a reason, and the fastest way to discover your purpose is to ask Him. He will answer. He just may not answer how or when you want. Just keep seeking. You will not feel confident in your purpose or the direction of it without a definite confirmation from God. All the steps discussed above will help move you toward your purpose. It's like God leaves a trail of breadcrumbs to bring us to the place of interaction with Him regarding His purpose for our lives.

I had a belief and a fuzzy sense of what my life might be about, but things got progressively clearer as I prayed about it. At some point in 1996, through prayer I sensed that I'd be developing people and that I would leave Nigeria at some point. This was a picture of my future, and it did not mean I should start implementing things immediately. Again, the important next step is prayer and intimacy with God. When He shows you something about your future, He often wants your belief and acceptance first. Trying to bring God's plan to pass in our own strength and time is an exercise in futility. Prayer and intimacy develop into trust and dependence. I had the courage to leave for Zambia in 1998 because of what I learned through prayer in 1996. The same was true with my decision to move to America in 2001.

Prayer will get you and keep you on the path of your purpose. The fulfillment will take a longer time, but there is joy in knowing you are on the right journey. Remember, the fulfillment of your purpose, though beneficial to you, is God's plan and His plan will be achieved. The big question is whether you'll be a willing and active participant or continue to live in disillusionment and dissatisfaction.

PREPARATION: Average Is Where We Start

"My life journey has been one of continual discovery. Some people have a vision of what they want to do from an early age; that wasn't me. I wanted to try many things, and still feel the urge to, but over the years, I've come to realize that my purpose is to mentor and develop men in the business world using my abilities as a systematic problem solver. That may sound like a mouthful, but it simply means that it's easy for me to visualize and understand how large systems work, identify where the problems are, and how to fix the issues. It's also easy for me to develop systems that make processes run smoother."

Noel Coleman became president of Connect Healthcare in 2014 after sixteen years at the company. He joined the company as a sales rep in 1998 when they were still a small start-up company. At the time of this writing (2020), this was the only company he had worked for, and in hindsight, it was the ideal place for him to develop as he has.

"I've always been an intense and driven person, and it often comes off as aggression and sometimes selfishness. I also had to face the harsh truth that I'm just an average guy—ouch! Still hurts to say that. I had the good fortune of working for a CEO who saw past my rough edges. He took me under his wing and mentored me; he gave me the opportunity to try things, to fail, to learn from them, and to keep growing. I realize now that being average is okay; it's where we all start out. But we should keep developing and growing ourselves. That's what my CEO did for me. I don't think most people or companies would have had that patience. I eventually succeeded him as president of the company. Those sixteen years under him were really preparation for what I get to do now."

Noel's story is not unique; the preparation phase is critical to fulfilling your purpose. The lives of musical prodigies and athletes really depict the importance of preparation in the fulfillment of purpose. In my second book, *DNA of Talent*, I write in detail about the importance of nurturing our talents before they can be put to good use. Wolfgang Amadeus Mozart, for example, wrote his first composition at the age of five. As remarkable as this was, the piece he wrote was not good enough to be performed for the public. His father, Leopold, saw and began nurturing the gift in his son and his older sister, Nannerl (who started taking piano lessons from their father at age seven and when Wolfgang was three),[1] and embarked on a European tour with the prodigies playing to many royal courts. Lessons with his father, playing to the different courts, meeting and learning from various more experienced musicians as they traveled, all summed up, can be seen as his preparation for his time. Most of Mozart's famous compositions were written after the age of twenty-five.

This cycle of discovery, preparation, and fulfillment plays out in nature. If you look at plants, you'll see that maturity will always precede fruit and flower production. This plays out in the animal kingdom as well. For humans, the preparation phase of our purpose journey will take many forms and may sometimes seem like we have strayed off the right path. This phase will include periods of formal and informal education, work experience, skill development, disappointments, maybe even life tragedies, along with exposure to different people and environments, etc. We will often forget that there is a bigger purpose to our lives as we get caught up in the day-to-day issues we have to deal with and will often wonder if our current circumstances have any meaning in the grand purpose. This temporary ambiguity is one of the frustrating aspects of seeking and discovering your purpose. It is also another reason why we need to depend on God and seek His guidance through prayer. What may feel like pain, disappointment, and failure today may turn out to be a necessary part of nudging you into the next phase of your purpose journey. No one is ever thrilled about being laid off from their job, but for some, this becomes the catalyst for starting a small business which eventually grows into a very large enterprise. All the ups and downs of their past have led up to this moment with the lessons learned now becoming practical tools they use.

Belief also plays a critical role in the preparation phase, because what you believe, is the reality you will live. This is not only a religious premise, it is a life principle, and one that holds true no matter what you believe or think. Many books have been written on the power of our thoughts; *Think and Grow Rich* and *The Magic of Thinking Big* are two of the well-known classics on this topic. Holding on to the belief that you are on your purpose journey will keep you on the right path, no matter how often you feel like you've strayed off, or when you go through something that just rocks your world and doubts begin to creep in. Stay positive and hold on to your belief. What works for me is remembering God's promise to me and meditating on Psalm 138, verse 8, which says, *"The Lord will fulfill* **His purpose** *for me; your steadfast love, O Lord, endures forever"* (NLT).

The purpose you carry is for a certain time. And until that time comes, you'll be in the preparation phase. The timing of the fulfillment of our purpose is not in my hands or your hands, because our scope of life is very limited. Each life is connected to so many other lives, and we can't fully grasp the interconnections and effects of each person's life. Only God has the capacity to see it all. Stay the course.

FULLFILLMENT: The Paradox of the Journey

For we are God's masterpiece. He has created us anew in Christ Jesus, so we can do the good things He planned for us long ago.
~ Ephesians 2:10 (NLT)

With the steps I've outlined above, you would think that the fulfillment of our purpose is a destination, a place or phase at which we arrive and get to use all our God-given abilities. Well . . . not exactly. Herein lies the paradox of the purpose journey—fulfilling your purpose is not a destination. It is a journey, a process.

Fulfilling (as in achieving) God's plan for your life is not just about doing something. It's more about becoming something. Who you become is more important to God than what you get to do. Really, God can do what He wants without us. His chief aim is making us more like Jesus. This is the true foundation of purpose. Rick Warren's bestseller *The Purpose Driven Life* delves deep into this.

You start to live out your purpose when you start searching for your purpose. And fulfillment (as in inner satisfaction) begins when we start making the course correction off the wrong path. This was the case for all those whose stories were told in this book; the fulfillment of purpose didn't happen when they got to a certain job, but when they realized something unique about how they were wired, and then started to pursue that more. They were growing in their character and in their professional acumen.

Working in your purpose is not about being famous or glamorous or even wealthy, but about deriving your deepest satisfaction by doing what you were designed to do on this side of eternity. It's not about how many likes, views, or awards you receive, it's about using your innate abilities to impact the world around you. That world may be your family, your company, your neighborhood, your city, or another country.

Many people sabotage the positive impact of their lives because they look for fame and measure their success based on how others respond to them. This is a recipe for failure and disappointment. We can't really control the outcome or the response of others to our purpose; we are only responsible for giving the best of ourselves. People are fickle and weird. Seriously, we are such oddballs with the capacity for strange mood swings. If the best of us still experience emotional yo-yo rides, how can you expect the rest of us to be consistent with how we feel and respond toward each other? We live in a society that is driven by fads and constantly looking for the next new thing so that we can move on from the former new thing.

When you settle into your purpose, don't get sidetracked by trying to be the new fad or remain hot. Stay focused on getting better at what you do, and those who need you will come to you. *Your purpose is not a fad; it's your assignment on the earth.*

RECAP:

The process of working in your purpose goes through three phases:
1. Discovery
2. Preparation
3. Fulfillment

The exercise in the next chapter will guide you through the steps of putting your purpose to work.

CHAPTER ELEVEN

The 7-Step Process to Working in Your Purpose

f you've worked through the exercises in previous chapters, you should have unearthed a lot of valuable information about yourself. Now it's time to use what you've learned to find a job where you can live out your purpose. I hope you've been writing your thoughts down in a journal; you'll need everything you've written.

This seven-step process will help you connect the dots and move in the direction of your ideal job. Each step has action steps and something for you to learn as you read. Don't rush through it. This will take some time and effort, but it is well worth it. You are worth it.

Step 1: Mine Your Answers

In reviewing your answers from all the chapter exercises, what theme(s) seem to keep recurring? Give yourself time to introspect and connect with what you may be feeling on the inside. Write your answers in your journal.

_____

_____

_____

This step is critical because it will reveal a lot about you. Like I said, God leaves us breadcrumbs; you can't hide from how you are wired. There are things you may have thought about, been drawn to, or often wished you could do for a long time, but you never saw them as something from which you could earn a living. And that is often the obstacle—this "earning a living" thought often short-circuits our thinking, probing, and even praying about pursuing work based on our natural abilities and purpose. You can earn a good living doing almost anything, if you know and have access to the people who need what you have to offer.

Step 2: Pray about It

You already know my belief, so this won't come as a surprise to you. God wants you to fulfill His purpose for your life. It's more important to Him than it is to you; seeking His guidance can only work in your benefit. I have yet to meet a person working in their divine purpose who did not pray for guidance, and they still do.

Step 3: Dream about It

In my career-coaching sessions, I guide my clients through a "Dream Career" exercise. This will help you mentally walk through the process of putting your thoughts into action. It's also powerful because it's non-threatening; all you are doing is engaging your imagination. I'll walk you through the process below.

"Dream Career" Exercise

Knowing what you now know about yourself—abilities, personality, interests, recurring life themes, desired industry, etc.—come up with two to three dream jobs/careers in which you get to spend most of your time working based on how you are wired. Assume you have total control over what you'll do at work and how you work. What would you do? Describe each job in as much detail as possible.

_____

_____

_____

_____

Remember, this is a dream, so don't limit yourself; let your inner child loose. You'll be amazed at what you come up with. Dreams are free, so go for it. DREAM AWAY!

Step 4: Define the Value You Bring

To understand why this step is important, let me first state why corporations exist. Corporations (or companies) exist to provide a service or a product for a profit. Corporations do not exist to create jobs; that is not their priority. Jobs are created in order to provide their service or product at a profit. You must embrace this reality in order to align with it. Your value to any organization is simply based on the role you play in helping them provide their service or product at a profit. And please note that profit can be based on increasing revenue, decreasing expenses, or extracting more value from the team.

You must answer the value question. Most people, unfortunately, cannot qualify and quantify the value they bring to their organization. If you can't qualify the value you bring, you'll most likely be undervalued. When you know the value you can offer an organization, you stop looking for a job and instead start looking for where you can add immense value. This is a mind shift.

The Value Equation

There are three components to defining your value:

1. Your strengths or natural abilities
2. Your role/position in the company
3. The mission or priorities of the organization

Write out each component separately. With these key pieces of information, you can write what I call your value proposition statement, or VPS. This statement will outline how your strengths and abilities make you valuable in the job you do to help your organization fulfill its mission.

Example of a value proposition statement:

My talents for connecting with people, teaching, and seeing emerging trends serve my company in my role as sales director as I work with my sales teams, coaching them where they need help and spotting opportunities to increase service to current and new clients.

With this understanding, ask yourself, "How will my dream jobs add value to the company I want to work for?"

_____

_____

_____

_____

Work through this step patiently; don't rush it. Ask questions like:

- What is the mission of the company I want to work for? What are their current priorities?
- Why is this role critical to the success of the company?
- What tasks/functions are critical in this role?
- How do and which of my natural abilities make me a good fit for this role?

Ask and answer these questions along with others which may occur to you.

Now write a statement that shows your match and value for this position. Trust me, you'll have to write and edit your VPS many times before it sounds right.

_____

_____

_____

Step 5: Test the Dream

This is where the rubber meets the road. Go online to Google or LinkedIn and search for people in the jobs you've been dreaming about. Use search terms or phrases you used in describing the job. You will find that there are people already doing exactly what you dreamed of, or very close to it. This step reveals the possibility of you working in your dream job. When you realize there are people getting paid to do what you want to do, you stop doubting and instead start exploring the possibility of making the dream a reality.

There may be other internal objections that arise, thoughts that pop up to tell you this isn't for you or that you aren't qualified or good enough for this position. That's why I had you write your value proposition statement first. Based on your strengths, you now have a better idea of the value you bring. Dispel the negative thoughts with the value you know you can bring.

In your journal, write down as many descriptions of your desired job that you find on the internet. Use this time to learn about the job. Are there any online groups for this job? What skills and experience are required for the job? Yes, I said skills. Remember that skills are an asset when they support your strengths.

This is how you test the dream jobs and make them more realistic and attainable.

Step 6: Connect with Someone

Now it's time to move from imagining to connecting with someone working in your dream job. The online research gives you head knowledge which, though useful, will not give you the day-to-day details of what it's like working in the job. Your research will prepare you to have a more productive meeting when you connect with people in the job; it'll help you ask more in-depth questions about the job—what it entails, what you need to learn, and even things you may need to avoid.

Things to Consider

1. Make a list of at least six people in your dream career and ask to meet with them. This is where you mine your network and ask for introductions. You can meet in person for coffee or lunch, virtually, or talk over the phone. Don't be afraid of people turning down your request. It'll happen, but if you are persistent you will find a few who will say yes.

2. Simply say that you are exploring a career in their field and you would like to learn more about the daily tasks and priorities of the job.

3. Prepare questions to ask ahead of time. Don't just show up and wing it.

4. At the meeting, ask about their priorities on the job, their strengths and abilities, what they love about the work, their daily routine on the job, what they want to change, what you may need to learn if you pursue this path, etc.

Step 7: Take Action

At this point, you should have all the information you need to make a transition. Don't be your stumbling block; commit to the process and take action.

TAKING ACTION is the only way to get into your career sweet spot. Don't give up on yourself. DON'T QUIT till you move into the position you want. Choose two to three people who will hold you accountable. Tell them the specific actions you want to take and dates by which you want to act on them. You control the action and not the outcome. However, if you don't take action, you won't see any positive outcome.

Some Action Steps

1. Review and revise your résumé. You should update it with your value proposition statement.

2. You may consider working with a résumé consultant who specializes in writing strengths-based résumés. It's worth investment, as they revise your past positions to reflect how your strengths have been used in the past.

3. Start talking with recruiters and be specific with what you are looking for.

4. Don't overlook the fact that the position you want may already exist within your current organization. If the opportunity is there, explore the possibility of making a shift.

5. If the position doesn't exist and you can show the value of why it should, based on how it will help the organization achieve its mission, increase profit, and/or reduce expenses, then prepare a case study and present it to your boss or the decision maker at your company.

6. If you don't have to, DO NOT leave your current job till you find your new desired position.

We Need Your Purpose

Living and working in your purpose requires submission to God as the One to whom we are ultimately responsible. And I'd like to end this book with a story that drives home the importance of identifying how you are wired, and letting that guide you through prayer, in the work you do and positions you take.

Purpose in Technology Sales

I've known Gerry Baron for almost twenty years, and this guy is great at selling. But he didn't fit the stereotypical mode of the gregarious salesperson.

"My purpose is to serve people by helping them apply technology to solve their complex business problems. I've spent most of my career in sales, but I don't really see myself as a salesperson. I love technology and genuinely want to help people apply technology in the best way to improve their businesses. The way my brain works, I am able to intuitively connect the dots between a client's description of problems they are trying to solve with

the capabilities of the solution I offer. People end up buying my solution because I identified their core issues and provided the right solution to meet it. I'm just deeply committed to solving my client's problems, and I'm constantly praying and asking God to show me how to best serve my clients and my company."

Yes, he prays. Gerry is a C-level sales executive who has obviously found his sweet spot in providing complex enterprise software solutions to his clients. At the time of our interview, he had held numerous senior positions at eleven different organizations. No matter what type of technology he sold, the constant theme which stood out was his ability to connect the dots between what his clients really needed and how his solution solved their issue. This type of selling requires more conceptual thinking and stakeholder coordination skills than transactional sales. Gerry is aware and confident in his abilities, but knows he serves a higher purpose and is constantly praying and asking God for wisdom and insight.

Gerry graduated from MIT in 1985 with a degree in mechanical engineering and computer science and landed his first job with Rabbit Software Corporation as a programmer.

"My foray into sales happened in 1988. I had been promoted to manage our European tech support operation. Our distributors and end users were having a hard time using our software. From talking with them, we realized that although the software capabilities were what they needed, the user interface was incompatible with European keyboards and characters because it had been designed in an American context. My team ended up developing local plugins to fix the issue for customers in each country we served. Our sales and customer satisfaction increased due to our responsiveness to the needs of the customers."

This experience taught Gerry the value of being customer centric.

"I realized that by really listening to the clients and understanding their key issues and the impact of those issues, being knowledgeable enough to recognize how my solution fit, being candid in my communication with them, and by setting realistic expectations, people trusted me, and more importantly, bought from me. This has been my approach to serving clients throughout my career and has consistently led to dramatic increase in sales revenue for the organizations I've worked for."

Gerry's story emphasizes the truth about purpose or calling; it is simply what you believe God has wired you to do. In his case, it is helping businesses apply the right technology solutions to their problems. Technology? Sales? God? Yes. How does this serve God or build His Kingdom? We may never fully know, but Gerry has had a positive influence in the lives of many of his employees and clients. The excellence with which he works opens the door for deeper personal conversations that go beyond work.

You were created by God for a purpose. Your purpose is not a job or a goal, but your purpose will be expressed through work. This book is focused on helping readers live out their purpose in and through their work, as in a calling expressed in a job. The fundamental truth about purpose is that "we were made by God for God, and to be like God" (refer to Genesis 1:26–28 for proof). Since there is no specification of what work we are to do, it makes sense to realize He includes all work in this directive. And all work means all work that has been, all work that currently is, and all work that is yet to be. Working in our purpose is expressed in every legal and moral profession imaginable—salespeople, scientists, pilots, mathematicians, computer programmers, graphic designers, construction workers, waiters, etc. Purpose is not just about the work we do, but how we let God use us in and through the work we do.

In the fulfillment of your purpose, your influence increases as others take note of not just what you do, but how you live. If you don't believe in God, then you most likely won't believe in life after death; maybe you think this life is all there is, and when you die, that's it. Well, that isn't true.

There is life after death, and this life is sort of a dress rehearsal for the true eternal life that exists beyond our present existence.

The famous line by Maximus in the movie *Gladiator*—"Brothers, what we do in life echoes in eternity"—is a truth, not just a cute movie quote. When I live out my purpose, I help others connect with and live out theirs.

You are how you are for why you are. Identify your how so you can fulfill your why. We need you and what you have to offer.

Purpose-to-Career Workshop

I nterested in working through this process with a coach? Join our live, virtual, seven-week Purpose-to-Career Workshop. Participants will have access to the Highlands Ability Battery, which is one of the most in-depth ability-assessment tools available today. You will work with an experienced coach in a cohort of twenty people max.

Session Outline

SESSION 1: HAB Assessment Debrief

Participants will take and finish the assessment prior to session starting. Your coach will spend this time giving you a deeper understanding of what your results mean. This assessment is the foundation of the work you'll do over the remaining weeks.

SESSION 2: Ideal Work Types and Environment

Participants will learn how to identify the ideal work roles and work environments they need to choose the ideal career path.

SESSION 3: Define My Purpose

Participants will learn how to mine their past for recurring patterns that point to their purpose. They will work through the process, learning how to use action verbs to articulate their purpose statement.

SESSION 4: Peer Feedback

Participants will work in group of four or five to help each member probe and sharpen their purpose statement. The peer sessions have been valuable in helping participants gain clarity on their purpose.

SESSION 5: Skills, Interests, and Value Definition

Participants will learn how to qualify the unique value they bring to an employer and define their value proposition statement.

SESSION 6: Career Visualization/Dream Exercise

Participants will be guided through a career visualization exercise which will teach them how to turn their dream career into reality.

SESSION 7: Activate Your Purpose

Participants will learn how to clearly state what their purpose means to the world they serve. This brings your purpose to specific action steps.

To register for a session, visit www.talentrevolution.me

Notes

Introduction

1. The Gallup organization is a global analytics and advice firm that helps leaders and organizations solve their most pressing problems. They conduct and publish the results of an annual survey of employees in the workforce to measure their engagement at work.

Chapter 1

1. Shakespeare, William. Pastoral comedy, *As You Like It*.
2. Warren, Rick. *The Purpose Driven Life*. Zondervan, 2002.
3. Johnson O'Connor Research Foundation. About Johnson O'Connor. https://www.jocrf.org/about/history.

Chapter 2

1. Csikszentmihalyi, Mihaly. Flow: *The Psychology of Optimal Experience*. Harper Collins, 2008.
2. Frankl, Victor E. *Man's Search for Meaning*. Beacon Press, 2006.

Chapter 3

1. One laptop per child experiment in Ethiopia. www.fastcompany.com/2681011/ethiopian-kids-hacked-their-donated-tablets-in-just-five-months (www.onelaptopperchild.org).

Chapter 4

1. Covey, Stephen R. *The 7 Habits of Highly Effective People*. Simon & Schuster, 1989.

Chapter 6

1. Maslow's hierarchy of needs. www.simplypsychology.org/maslow.
    html.

Chapter 10

1. Greene, Robert. Mozart family story in *Mastery*. Penguin Books,
    2012.

My Kickstarter Backers

It's one thing to write a book and another thing to publish it, especially during a pandemic. The publishing expenses were covered with the help of my dear friends whose names appear below. 2020 was a crazy year due to the pandemic and these rock stars helped get us over the finish line. I am indebted to each of you and I deeply appreciate your belief in the project and your partnership with me. Thank you very much.

Aaron Grijalva
Adeoye Oguntomilade
Adetayo Adewolu
Alex Lakanu
Amanda Mataski
Amanda Price
Ami Scott
Amy Balogh
Ashley Puccini
Aubrey Augenstein
Audrius Stripeikis
Biola Adeniyi
Caroline Jalango
Dani Sanabria
Daniel Skrok
De'Arlo Bennett-Bracy
Dianne Young
Elisa M. Cupani
Emily Shinn
Ginger Clopper
Gladys Watanabe
Heartistry LLC
Henry Nwokolo
Ify Akpuaka
Isoken Aiwerioba
James Donnelly
Jana Barnhill
Jason Liles
Jeanne Sheahan
Johanna Asher
Judith McKenzie

Julie Lindsay
Katherine Muriithi
Katherine Patchett
Kathleen Hill
Kim Cunningham
Lana S. McFarlane
Lee Holliday
Marilyn Ringo
Meghan Riley
Michelle McBurney Hanchey
Mona Cooper
Monica Elliott
Nancy Vason
Nata Lia
Ngozi Onyejekwe
Okoroafor Maduagwu
Oluwole Coker
Raphael Madu
Reece Carter
Rizu Nwokoma
Ronald Jones
Rotimi Balogun
Sarah Rosson
Shae Owens Holley
Sibyl Slade
Tayo Adeyeye
The Creative Fund by BackerKit
The Pate Pack
Victoria Teague
Warren and Tiffany Little
Zane Nolte

About the Author

Kene Iloenyosi teaches Gens X, Y, and Z how to discover and work in their purpose. He knows what it feels like to be unfulfilled in the work you do even when you are being well paid. He's been there and he made it out. He now uses his natural abilities of teaching, connecting, and communicating to guide others to a fulfilling career path.

He is the author of *Finding Your Sweet Spot* and *DNA of Talent*, and through his coaching company, Talent Revolution, he conducts virtual workshops where participants learn how to discover their purpose and put it to work.